Warrior In Two Worlds

Healing From Broken Ways
Finding True Identity

Don Standing Bear Forest

ISBN 978-1-958788-26-4 (digital)

ISBN 978-1-958788-27-1 (paperback)

ISBN 978-1-958788-28-8 (hardcover)

Copyright © 2022 by Don Standing Bear Forest

All Rights Reserved. No part of this publication may be reproduced, distributed, or transmitted in any form or by any means, including photocopying, recording, or other electronic or mechanical methods without the prior written permission of the publisher. For permission requests, solicit the publisher via the address below.

Publify Publishing

1412 W. Ave B

Lampasas, TX 76550

publifypublishing@gmail.com

Dedication

To those who struggle with broken ways, as do we all.

ACKNOWLEDGEMENTS

Writing this book was a tall task, which would not have been possible had it not been for the promptings, encouragement, and support of many people along the way.

I owe a debt of gratitude to my providers in the medical and healing fields, to my Native brothers and sisters, to my teachers and mentors in recovery, and to my ministry brothers and sisters who have challenged and inspired me to learn the importance of a personal relationship with the God of my understanding.

My thanks also go to the young adults I have had the honor and privilege to work with for several years.

I feel humbled and blessed by all who, by their example and words, have influenced the man I have become.

My wife, Edie, has been my best friend and supporter during this project. She has been an exceptional caregiver as she walked with me through all the years of chronic pain, surgeries, and bouts of severe depression over the 35 years of our journey together. Edie also helped with editing this manuscript and kept encouraging me when I stumbled. Wela'lioq (thank you/Mi'kmaq) My Love.

My dad, Andre Grey Wolf, and I had a special relationship. He was the example of humility and generosity to others, no matter who they were. He and my mom, Esther Night Dancer, loved children and young adults. They raised five children of their own, and 68 foster babies from the age of five days old until they were adopted months later. Mom had more love to give than her small frame could hold. Wela'lin (thank you/plural/Mi'kmaq)

Love and appreciation go out to my mentors and writing coaches, Greg and Tara, for getting me focused, through their encouragement and practical advice along this journey of writing. Wela'lioq

My natural brother, Skippy, passed on before I was born. Therefore, I had no brother in my youth. If I could choose a brother, it would be Gary. He and his wife (my "sister") Mindy will always be a part of my life. Mindy also helped edit this manuscript and shared her honest feedback. Wela'lioq

For the wisdom of Chief Flying Eagle, Chief Roland, and Chief Peter John, Wela'lioq

To Lynn Chiwabiinonquay (Strong East Wind Woman) Bessette, for mentoring, and eventually partnering with me, in the artform of Wampum weaving, and passing on to me the title of "Master Wampum Weaver."

To artist friends and supporters Bud, Yolanda and Ron, Shane, Papahone, Cliff, Judy and Roger, Dixie and Cindy, and the rest of my extended family of artists, Wela'lioq

To my spiritual mentors and brothers and sisters, Pat and Jim, Ken, Scott, Mark D, Tricia, Heather, Wendy, Tristin, John, Byron, and Curtis, Wela'lioq

To my Native American Jesus Way mentors, brothers and sisters, Richard Twiss, Doug, Bill, Guy, Sequilla, Jerry, Larry, and Jonathan. Wela'lioq

To my physical healing team, Dr. Beth, Dr. Cary K, Dr. David J, and Dr. Ron M, Wela'lioq

To my literary agent Amanda, Wela'lioq

And especially to Geesuk (Creator, in my Mi'kmaq language) Yeshua, for redeeming my life, and allowing me to share these stories of your healing work, so that others may have hope. Wela'lin. I am Yours.

Table of Contents

FORWARD BY CURTIS IVANOFF 1

FORWARD BY GREG HINTZ 3

AUTHOR'S NOTE 5

PROLOGUE 8

LIQUID SUICIDE 8

INTRODUCTION TO WARRIOR IN TWO WORLDS 11

CHAPTER ONE - SPIRITUAL (the soul) 14

    UNCONDITIONAL LOVE 15

    "WHO ARE YOU" 17

    "WE HAVE TO STOP" 20

    THE MISSING PIECE 24

    UNEXPECTED MESSENGERS 27

CHAPTER TWO - EMOTIONAL (The Heart) 30

    "NEVER BELONGING" 31

    THE ABYSS 35

    CARRYING A GRUDGE 37

    ALL YOUR FAULT 41

    MY FATHER'S EYES 46

    IS GOD LIKE MY DAD? 48

CHAPTER THREE - MENTAL (the mind) 59

    A SECOND CHANCE 60

    METLAKATLA 67

    GETTING OUT OF THE BOX 76

CHAPTER FOUR: - PHYSICAL (strength) 79
    SOLUTIONS TO PAIN 80
    MYSTERIOUS MALADY 86
    THIS VESSEL 91
CHAPTER FIVE - VISION QUEST 94
OUTRO 102
OUT OF DARKNESS TO LIGHT 102
RETREAT 104
PONDERISMS 106
SELECTED PRAYERS 108
A NOTE ON THE COVER DESIGN 113
EPILOGUE 114
FOOTNOTES 115
BIBLIOGRAPHY 116

FORWARD

BY CURTIS IVANOFF

I was once in a small western Alaska village where I went to visit an elder who was a leader in the local church. As I approached his house on a cold January morning, I could not help but notice this tall carving of a bear standing in front of their house. It was a huge tree trunk on which the man had used a chainsaw to turn it into this image. Of course, I took a selfie with the bear before I went inside. I commented to the man how neat it was, and then he shared the story of how it came to be. He was on the beach with his wife in the fall, taking a ride on their four-wheeler. He stopped when he saw the tree trunk, amazed by its size. He told his wife that he wanted to bring it to their house. He had an idea. He gathered some young men and a trailer and hauled it home. Over the course of the fall he began to work on his idea, what eventually became this bear.

"When I saw the wood on the beach, I imagined it right away, a bear. I could see it in my mind's eye," he told me with his eyes closed and hand outstretched as he recreated the moment of inspiration for me. I complimented him on his handiwork and asked him how he did it.

"Well, it's pretty simple. I got my chainsaw and began to remove anything that wasn't a bear." I thought to myself, there is a spiritual message in that.

> *For we are God's workmanship, created in Christ Jesus, to do good works which God has prepared in advance for us to do.*
>
> Ephesians 2:10

Don's story is like that. Jesus saw a young lost man, confused, and dazed by alcohol. What we read here is a writing style that, just like Don himself, is very inviting. What we will see is the same thing that Jesus could see in his mind's eye…not a bear, but Don Standing Bear, fully redeemed and made alive by him, now living the way God had created him to be.

We see how God used, not a chainsaw, but relationships such as with Edie, to help form and shape this man, once he had been made alive by Christ. Don offers a wonderful gift to give us a glimpse of grace and a story of hope in the telling of his life journey.

Don Standing Bear is an artist. I have seen his pieces of artwork and they are beautiful. His handiwork reflects a part of his journey as he shares his struggles of wrestling with identity. In reading his story, I could not help but think of this passage in Ephesians 2 where the author used a powerful image to tell the followers of the Jesus Way in Ephesus who they were – God's workmanship. Together, collectively as a community, those people reflected a new people God had called and formed through the love and grace of Jesus. In that passage we read that they had been brought from death to life. It is quite a contrast of realities. What we find in Don's story is a testimony of this creative and transformational power of Jesus Christ.

Curtis Ivanoff,

Inupiaq name "Yungaq"

Superintendent of the Alaska Covenant Conference

FORWARD

BY GREG HINTZ

I still remember the moment we were sitting in this restaurant and began talking about a dream that Don had. It wasn't a dream that was placed there as he slept, but it was a dream that was alive and living deep within him. It was a message that he had to get out. It was something that had to be shared. He started to talk about this dream to my wife and I and you could feel the electricity in the room.

What Don began to share with us was rich and deep. It was a clear understanding about life that had only come through difficulty, struggle, and perceived failure. However, it was the culmination of those dark seasons that had created something new and beautiful in his heart. It was a way of looking at life that honored his rich faith and the culture that was so close to his heart.

After hearing his heart, a moment of silence followed. Then I heard the words of my wife. "What are you waiting for? It sounds like you already have something great to share."

These words were like the starting gun of a race as this book really took flight in that moment. There was writing and praying and discussions and revisions and all the things that make for an incredible book. And then, the beloved launch.

Now I find myself standing at the finish line in awe of what has been created. Words that are real, thought provoking, challenging, and engaging. These words that you are about to read were birthed in these moments and now have found their way into your life.

With that, I want to encourage you on this journey. Don has poured his heart out onto these pages. Through anger, tears, hope and pain, Don has written words to assist us on the journey of life. With each step we get closer and closer to our own destination… to our own healing.

May the Creator of all things whisper to your soul on this journey, calling you into a deeper relationship with your life. The Creator's plan is perfect. Humbly submit to this plan in your life and watch what God will do.

Greg Hintz

Lover of life and Jesus.

Husband, Dad, Pastor, Coach and Friend.

Change IS Possible

AUTHOR'S NOTE

Over a period of years, various random people had asked me to write about my experiences and lessons learned over the course of my life.

I would always respond, "It's just my life and what I have experienced, no big deal."

But the messengers kept appearing:

- I was taken aback at her unexpected statement, "I know the introduction for your book."

We had just entered her office. She sat down and repeated the statement that took me off guard again, "I know what you need to write for the introduction to your book."

At our last visit, my naturopathic doctor had encouraged me to start writing this book and pointed out how influential it could be in helping others to heal and find purpose in their lives, but I did not know how to begin.

Now she explained, "Write about why you feel it is so difficult. What are you afraid of? And remember it is not about you; it is about what your Creator God has done for, and through you, for others."

- As I opened the door to the art gallery of my friend, mentor, and teacher, she turned to greet me with, "I know the title of the book you will write."

I looked away embarrassed, thinking to myself, "No one's going to want to read it; why does everyone keep bringing it up?" I have since learned that many people do want to read it and I needed to write it so they could!

- I was exhibiting my artwork at a holistic show. Another exhibitor came over and introduced herself to me, and we struck up a conversation. She wrote on a piece of paper and handed it to me and walked off. I had never seen her before and have never seen her since. I unfolded the note to read, in bold letters, "WRITE YOUR BOOK!"
- I was selling my artwork during the Indian Marketplace Show, at the Autry Museum in Los Angeles. A couple had been spending a good deal of time at my booth, looking intently at my jewelry, carvings, and wampum.

This couple then walked over to where I was sitting and asked, "Have you written your book yet?"

I sheepishly replied, "No, but others have asked me that, too."

My wife elbowed me in the ribs to let me know she had also heard this question from the couple we had never met before.

- My friend opened my laptop computer and booted it up. She was tired of asking me if I had started on "The Book". I am not very skilled in computer technology, and I would let her know this each time she asked that question. So, on this day, she proceeded to hit a few keys on the keypad and then turn the computer for me to see the screen, which now displayed a new icon with the caption "The Book".

She then informed me that I had no more excuses. "Just click on it, open it up, and start writing."

- My friend came to visit me at one of my shows. I had known this man for many years and had been a mentor and teacher to him.

We visited for a while, and then he got up from his chair, stood in front of me, grabbed my shirt collar, looked me in the eye from about 6 inches away, and proclaimed, "When are you going to write your damned book? You have helped so many of us, you can give hope to others by writing this book."

How many times did I need to be prodded? I had been running away from writing this book due to fear of failure. I was wandering in the spiritual wilderness, feeling aimless, stagnant, and useless, when a friend in Arizona said to me, "Perhaps you are in the wilderness because you are disobeying God." This truth struck me like a ton of bricks. She was right! Her statement inspired me to finally begin writing this book so many had been asking about.

I was once told that my past would become my greatest asset…my journey from the darkness of defeat and despair to the joy of living in the Sunlight of the Spirit could help others do the same. I have learned that my life is not really mine. I am alive today because of the gift of Life from Creator God, his mercy and grace. This book is stories of faith-building experiences, and the growth of a personal relationship with Creator God; not an "inside the box" religious experience, by any means.

Let me now take you on a journey from self-absorption to self-discovery, of becoming teachable, and embracing who Creator God made me to be, happy, joyous, and free.

"Deep down in every man, woman, and child, is the fundamental idea of God…" (1) the pain, brokenness, trauma, and insanity of our lives is constantly fighting this truth. So many of us struggle with this brokenness, disconnection, and disillusionment. If this is you, perhaps this book is for you. There is a solution. My hope is that this book will bring good news to those who have only heard bad news.

> *"Let the redeemed of the Lord tell their story, those he redeemed from the hand of the enemy, and gathered them out of the lands, from the east, west, north, and south."*
>
> Psalm 107:2

PROLOGUE

LIQUID SUICIDE

"Who has woe? Who has sorrow? Who has strife? Who has complaints? Who has needless bruises? Who has bloodshot eyes?... in the end, it bites like a snake, and poisons like a viper. Your eyes will see strange sights, and your mind will imagine confusing things... 'They hit me', you will say, 'but I am not hurt! They beat me, but I don't feel it! When will I wake up so I can find another drink?'"

Proverbs 23: 29-35

"Sometimes God lets you hit rock bottom so that you will discover that He is the rock at the bottom."

Dr. Tony Evans

It all began in the middle.

"Where am I? Am I alive? Oh no, how did I get home?" A sluggish awareness began setting in. My blurred eyes couldn't focus. Guilt, shame, devastating remorse... "Is my vehicle here? Did I hurt anyone? Who cares, what's the use! I am just a piece of crap; why am I even alive? No one cares."

I could not stand up. My legs would not function. Good thing for this old stinky mattress that was on the floor. All I could do was roll off it onto the stale booze-drenched old carpet. I attempted to get to my hands and knees unsuccessfully, and instead slithered across the rug. Liquid death was trying to envelop me.

My head dropped to the floor. I reflected on my current predicament, coming to after many days of continuous drinking, waking up from blackouts, finding myself in different establishments, homes and at the infamous Curling Bonspiel in Fairbanks. All this time I was driving from one place to the next. I participated in this craziness for years, too many years.

This experience of "coming to" was not a pleasant one, and the only solution I knew was more alcohol. I kept open cans of beer next to my mattress, so the carbonation would not cause me to vomit. My only salvation was to begin the cycle over again, leading to black outs or passing out. I knew no other way.

All I thought about was booze. Do I have enough? How do I get enough? It was my god.

Living this stagnant and erratic self-destructive lifestyle led me to seek out sordid places and people like myself, who called being continuously drunk "normal". I had visions of living under the Cushman Street bridge with the other homeless drunks, submerged in a continuous alcoholic stupor. I also envisioned moving into a cabin in the Bush accompanied by a massive supply of bottles of any kind. I even scouted out different locations. It was as if I was looking forward to the end.

I was broken, physically, emotionally, mentally, and spiritually. "No one understands. I'm not smart enough; I have no skills to speak of. I lost my relationships, but it's their fault. I'm unemployable. My body is broken and falling apart more and more. I'm a 100 mile an hour pile of junk. I'm just a drunken Indian ('The meanest in the valley,' Pride added). But I was overwhelmed by fear, self-loathing, self-pity, and no self-worth, near hopeless.

Little did I know right then, that as I lay prostrate on that dirty rug, this was to be the beginning of the end of my alcoholic way of progressive suicide.

As I tried to move my almost lifeless body, four words came from deep within me and formed a prayer, "God, please help me."

This was not like my usual bargain prayer, "If you get me out of this mess, I will never do this or that again." There was something desperately sincere about this prayer.

> *"Then they cried out to the Lord in their trouble, and he delivered them from their distress."*
>
> Psalm 107:6

INTRODUCTION TO WARRIOR IN TWO WORLDS

Prior to my prayer of desperation, I knew of only one world, a broken world. This world in which I lived was dark, hostile, angry, judgmental, dangerous, and lonely. I lived in fear, and I fought to survive in any way I could: blaming, using, controlling, and belittling those around me, plus using alcohol to numb my feelings of fear, guilt, remorse, hopelessness, and self-loathing. In this world, I projected the image of a tough- guy warrior who didn't care about anything and was unbeatable, but in reality, I was badly losing the war, and slowly dying, inside and out.

A glimmer of light from the second world, the world I had never seen, broke through the crack in my armor the day of that prayer. This book chronicles stories of my journey from death to life, from dark to light, from despair to joy, from being someone no one wanted to be around to someone with a myriad of friends and healthy relationships. In this new world there was nothing about me that was unredeemable. Even my ugly past became an asset to help others who are where I was. I became a warrior who defends and helps others. I found my true identity.

These two worlds still exist; the battle is not over, and the old one still tries to draw me back in one way or another at times. I remain a warrior in two worlds, as do we all. You will recognize the two worlds in these stories. May these stories inspire you in your walk along this road called life. Perhaps you are traveling the broken road and desire healing. If these amazing things can happen in my life, they can happen in yours. May you, too, find peace, joy, love, and your true identity along the good road. "Wela'lin msit no'kmaq" (Mi'kmaq) All my Relations; May you walk in beauty.

HEALING THROUGH THE MEDICINE WHEEL

> *"You (may) have noticed that everything an Indian does is in a circle, and that is because the Power of the World always works in circles, and everything tries to be round... The sky is round, and I have heard the earth is round like a ball, and so are the stars. The wind, in its greatest power, whirls. Birds make their nests in circles, for theirs is the same religion as ours. Even the seasons form a great circle in their changing, and always come back again to where they were. The life of a man is a circle, from childhood to childhood, and so it is in everything where power moves."*
>
> Black Elk, Oglala Sioux, 1863-1950

> *"Those he gathered from the lands, from east and west, from north and south."*
>
> Psalm 107:3

As my identity includes my First Nations heritage (Mi'kmaq; Abenaki, Huron), I have chosen to arrange my life stories according to one application of the Medicine Wheel (see illustration), with a focus on each of the spiritual, emotional, mental, and physical areas of challenges and growth. Each of these quadrants of our being interrelate, and when one is weak, engaging the others often helps. For example, when experiencing the emotion of sadness: deciding (mental), to take a walk in the woods (physical), and pray (spiritual), will likely prove helpful.

Here are my stories.

Native peoples of America recognize the wisdom of the circle, and also observed how many things appear in "4's. They use the circular medicine wheel with its four quadrants as a basic learning tool for this journey called life. Our Creator, Great Spirit, God, is the central power holding all elements of the medicine wheel together.

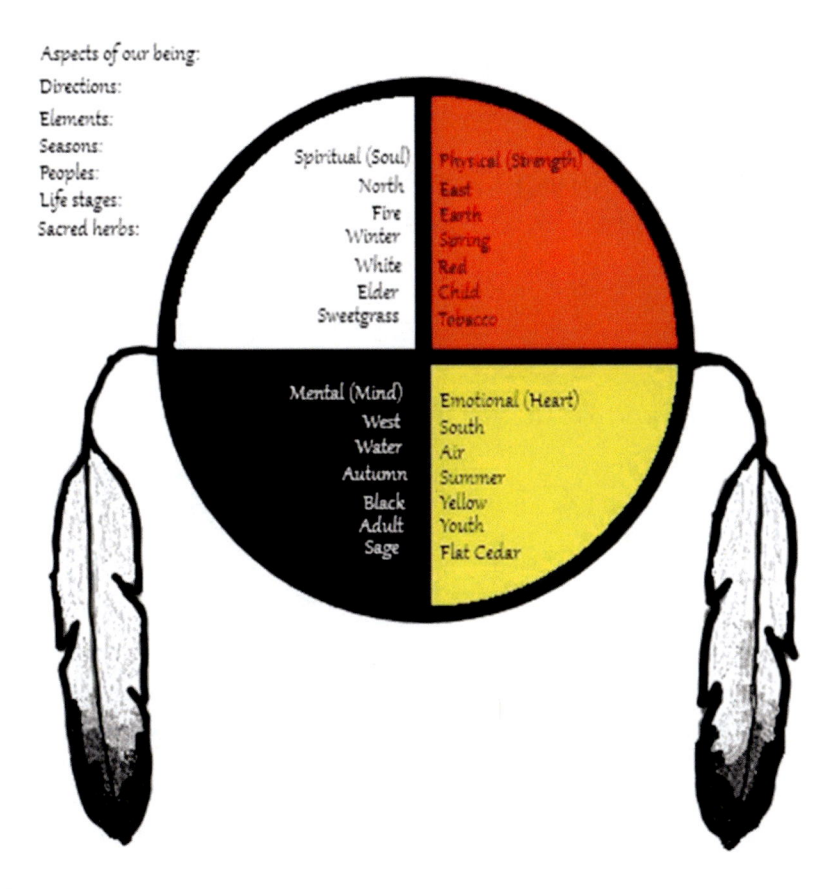

Aspects of our being:
Directions:
Elements:
Seasons:
Peoples:
Life stages:
Sacred herbs:

Spiritual (Soul)	Physical (Strength)
North	East
Fire	Earth
Winter	Spring
White	Red
Elder	Child
Sweetgrass	Tobacco
Mental (Mind)	Emotional (Heart)
West	South
Water	Air
Autumn	Summer
Black	Yellow
Adult	Youth
Sage	Flat Cedar

CHAPTER ONE

SPIRITUAL (the soul)

"Of or pertaining to the spirit or soul, as distinguished from the physical nature"

(2)

UNCONDITIONAL LOVE

"Love is something you and I must have. We must have it because our Spirit feeds upon it."

Chief Dan George, Coast Salish

1899-1981

Patricia and Jim accepted me....as drunk and flawed as a person could be. I had met them six years before my prayer of desperation. Jim and I would spend a great deal of time during those years, fishing, and looking for moose (hunting). During those day trips, with an occasional overnight at moose camp, he treated me like a brother. He knew I was "itchy" and couldn't wait to find my next drink. I did not actively drink on those excursions. One of the very few moral codes I adhered to was "alcohol and firearms don't mix". I was mostly hung over and/or craving the next drink whenever I was with Patricia and Jim, because that was my life.

As I continued to drink, I deteriorated further, spiraling down into the dark abyss of loneliness. No one wanted to be around me anymore, except for Jim and Patricia. They welcomed me into their home anytime I asked. Countless times after "coming to", following a drinking bout, I would call them up and ask to visit. They knew from my appearance what I had been doing. I was in pretty rough shape.

I would arrive at their home, and they would greet me in their matter-of-fact way. Patricia would hand me a glass of sweet tea, as if she knew I needed the sugar. A body addicted to alcohol (which is comprised of empty carbohydrates), craves more empty carbohydrates. I would be shaking and sweating profusely. They would go about their business and would check on me from time to time as I sat in their living room. They offered no lecturing, no belittling, no condemnation.

After a while, food would be offered. Sometimes I could eat; other times they knew I just couldn't handle the food and made something for me to take home.

I was aware that they didn't drink, and I also surmised that they had religion of some sort, but they allowed me the freedom necessary to "just be". I know now that they are Jesus Way people, and that they prayed for me a lot. I now also know that through their unconditional love, God drew me in. Even when I felt worthless, they saw worth in me. They genuinely loved me as Jesus loves.

This relationship with Patricia and Jim became one of the foundational building blocks in my spiritual growth.

"God is Love"

1 John 4:16

"WHO ARE YOU"

"Men must be born and reborn to belong"

Luther Standing Bear, Oglala Sioux

1868–1937

This was not normal for me. I was now sober. Alcohol, fear, and rage; that was my normal. I had lived in an alcoholic stupor for so many years to avoid the pain associated with having to deal with any form of reality. So, there I sat, laden down with the horrors of my past, minus my one coping mechanism, alcohol. That familiar empty feeling of despair was attempting to take hold of me once again.

This new and foreign way of living required guidance for me to survive and find my way. I have heard that when the student is ready, the teacher appears. A variety of people appeared, who were willing to nudge me along this path of healing, but one man in particular became my closest ally and spiritual guide through this walk. He assured me that he would be there to help in any way he could if I didn't drink. Early in my journey of sobriety, this man and I had spent hours talking and drinking coffee at a coffee shop in town and he agreed to mentor me in this new life. Standing in the foyer of the restaurant on our way out one day, he turned to ask me a simple but powerful question that changed the trajectory of my life.

"Who are you?" he asked. "I don't want to know your job, your race, your height, or any of that stuff."

I mused to myself, "What does he mean?"

Then he asked again, "Who are you?" I searched within and came up blank.

"I don't know." This was the first honest answer I ever gave. I truly did not know who I was, but it was something I needed to find out. All I had known were some not so flattering man-made labels I had accrued along the way, in addition to my own internal self-abasing, self-destructive beliefs. I would refer to myself as "A 100 mile per hour pile of junk." With such a foundation of guilt, remorse, and self-loathing, I never wanted to be myself. Rather, I fervently tried to imitate others. I wanted to be anybody but me. However, most of the characters I emulated were exactly that, "characters", for the most part, not the best role models.

Now I was on untrodden ground. Oddly enough, I found that to discover "who I am", I first needed to discover who God is. However, at this point in my life I would shudder at the mere mention of the word "God". I had an unhealthy distorted notion of who God was. I was convinced that He was angry and punitive, and I had done so much wrong in my life, I would always be on his bad side, so why try?

But the God that my guide spoke of and seemed to love so much, was quite different. My friend had peace and joy in his life and was comfortable in his own skin! He said, "if I continued on the sobriety path and was willing to do the work it would take, I could have what he had, and this was something I very much wanted."

He said, "This journey of being sober is not religious, but spiritual." In my confused state, I could not understand what he meant. But there was a degree of hope that my life would change, and I clung to this.

I did the work it took to find out who this Creator God truly was as he revealed Himself to me, and showed me who He made me to be; his beloved child, beautifully and wonderfully made, just as I am, but desiring to be more like Him all the time. Now this hope is passed on to others who I get to guide along the path of sobriety as they seek to answer the question "Who am I?" for themselves.

"WE HAVE TO STOP"

> *"Do not allow others to make your path for you. It is your road and yours alone. Others may walk it with you, but no one can walk it for you. Accept yourself and your actions. Own your thoughts. Speak up when wrong and apologize. Always know your path. To do this you must know yourself inside and out, accept your gifts as well as your shortcomings, and grow each day with honesty, integrity, compassion, faith, and brotherhood. I have made myself what I am."*
>
> Tecumseh, Shawnee, 1768-1813

Early in my journey of sober living, I had so many questions. All things were new. My guides had to teach me to relax and slow down. This was not easy and often uncomfortable. I became begrudgingly accustomed to them saying, "you're right where you are supposed to be." They usually shared this bit of wisdom while I was experiencing my various challenges in learning how to live. In my old life I only knew how to slowly die. During these confusing interludes, I still desired the sober life, and I needed these men and women's experience to guide me. I knew I could not do it alone. I saw in their lives and in their teachings how a Spirit-led life, directed by God, as I understood Him, would help solve all my problems.

Since I was a novice in anything relating to a Spirit-led life, I found it necessary to begin by trying to believe in their beliefs, though they were leading me, in time, to find my own. They used encouragement and inspiration along with tough love. They cut me little slack. This sobriety is a matter of life or death. At the time, I sometimes wondered why I was saved from such a hideous alcoholic death. I didn't know why. I was just grateful.

My mentors offered hope and compassion, as long as I was willing to do the footwork, and I was! I became hungry for this unfamiliar new way of life. I began to grow in my prayer life, seeking and searching, experiencing so much wonderment that life had to offer.

About a year into my sobriety, one man, who became my teacher, played a significant role in helping me find my own understanding of God…in a most unexpected way.

I admired this man's calm demeanor, how he spoke, and the wisdom he shared. We spent a lot of time together working on my spiritual growth and plan of action. At the time, I was also dealing with some pretty serious physical pain and legal issues associated with a work-related injury, so he got to see the best and the worst of me yet stayed the course. Unknowingly, I was leaning quite heavily on him to help me understand how to navigate this new life. I listened intently to how he felt about people, places, and things, religion, politics, you name it!

During one of our sessions, as he was assisting me on my written moral inventory, he put everything aside and bluntly stated, "We have to stop."

I was blindsided. "What???"

He said that the God he believed in, told him to stop. He didn't know why, just stop. We got on our knees and prayed. Then he left. I believed in this man so much that I went along with the guidance he received from his God....at first.

But over time, my frustration mounted, until it almost boiled over. I was confused and hurt as he spent less and less time with me. When we were around each other, I felt as if he was blocking me out. This lasted for about a year.

Other spiritual men were spending time with me over coffee and other social times.

Finally, I asked another man to be my guide.

His response was, "I would be honored to."

Wow! No one had ever said they would be honored to do anything for me before. I had known this man for a couple of years, and we spent time together, as he taught me how to enjoy life, mostly out in creation.

As he guided me back into working this moral inventory that had come to a screeching halt a year prior, I came to the man's name who "dumped" me, on my "resentments" list. I wrote after his name what I still felt: resentment, bitterness, envy, and self-chastisement. But as I continued to write about my part in it, a new insight was revealed as my pen wrote on the paper. I suddenly realized why he and I had to stop when we did.

Tears rolled down my cheeks onto the page, as I received this marvelous moment of clarity from my God. I found that my prior mentor's beliefs had become my beliefs in, and about everything! His understanding of God became my understanding. I was at that time relying on another man, rather than developing my own personal relationship with God.

My feelings and thoughts of resentment, hate, and bitterness vanished.

During a retreat we both later attended, and with that new sparkle in my eye, I asked him if we could have lunch together.

He looked at me and said, "Yes, indeed, I would enjoy that."

During lunch, I explained to him what had been revealed to me during my inventory. I also shared my appreciation and gratitude that he listened to his God about stopping. He said he knew that we had to stop, but he did not know why either. Now with my revelation, it made sense to him, and he was glad he listened, and stopped, despite not knowing why at the time.

Once I let go of my friend's view of God and everything else, I began to grow in my own understanding of God and develop a personal relationship with him, as I could not have done before. I also started to learn that there really was a "me" in there who could, with the help of my God, form my own healthy opinions and views. I wasn't at the time, but now I am grateful that "we had to stop."

THE MISSING PIECE

"Dance for joy at all times. Never stop sending up prayers. Give thanks to the Great Spirit in all things, for this is what he wants from you, as you dance in step with Creator Sets Free (Jesus), the Chosen One. Do not put out the fire of the Holy Spirit."

1 Thessalonians 5:16-19 (FNV)

I stopped in my tracks, frozen, as time stood still. I stood motionless, grasping the handrail at the top of the stairs. The sound of the Native drumbeat resonated with my inner being. At this time, in 1976, I was enrolled as a student at the University of Alaska Fairbanks, where the Festival of Native Arts was currently being held, with its various art forms, including Native drum and dance performances. I stood there for an indeterminate amount of time, as memories of my Native grandmother's words permeated my being.

When I was little, my grandmother would sit with my sister and me and share stories of our Native heritage. Her beautiful round face and wonderful spirit-filled eyes would glow as she spoke to us. But always at the end of our time, a solemn expression would overcome her face. She would place her index finger over her lips and say, "Shhh...we don't tell anyone." This was in the 1950s. I didn't tell anyone. I relegated her words to the far recesses of my mind.

Because of my life experiences, and being a "half-breed," I lacked the ability to fit in or belong.

The 1976 Festival of Native Arts produced the first crack in the walls I had built physically, emotionally, mentally, and spiritually. But I refused to let that crack widen enough to allow the light of my Native heritage to begin to shine through. I still spent many years wrestling with my identity as a human and drowned my struggles in the haze of alcohol. I could not function in school, and just stopped going to classes. "Incomplete" had more meaning in my life than just a word on a transcript.

Fast forward to 1988. My whole attitude and outlook on life had changed. No longer using alcohol, I had become teachable. I followed that long-repressed yearning to reconnect with my Native family. I called my dad and discovered that he desired to do the same thing! He shared what he knew of our heritage and ended up getting our official genealogy and eventually tribal membership for us. We were Mi'kmaq, Abenaki, Huron, Métis, and French-Canadian.

I also connected with my extended Native American and Alaska Native families in the Fairbanks area. In 1991, I graduated with degrees in Criminal Justice, and Sociology. My graduate work was done in Indian Law. However due to a chronic physical problem from a prior injury, I was unemployable, or as some had told me, an employment liability. I prayed for guidance about what to do with my life.

Meanwhile, my mom and dad shared our traditional Native art forms with me. Local Native artists, here in Alaska, encouraged me to pursue my creativity in the field of Native Art. I started carving moose and caribou bone, and antler pendants, for earrings and necklaces, and I incorporated other natural and organic materials into my pieces. These finished products were used as gifts for family and friends.

Then in 1996, while we were at moose camp, my friend/mentor/hunting partner said to me,

"Why don't you really spend time doing this art?"

I responded, "I can't even draw a stickman!"

His reply... "Creator God doesn't want you to draw a stickman."

Five months later I was accepted into my first Native Art show. It was the Festival of Native Arts show where, twenty years earlier, the drum had so moved my spirit. Since this first show, I have participated in major Indian art markets across North America, and have supplied galleries, stores, and museums with this gift of art which Creator God has given me. I have embraced the heritage that my grandmother introduced to me; an important part of the identity God blessed me with. I had the honor of receiving the name, "Standing Bear" at my naming ceremony. I participated in powwows, traditional gatherings, and tribal council meetings with my family, as well as attending Native Alaskan cultural events.

On suggestion from my Athabaskan friend, mentor, and teacher, Richard, and with approval from Athabaskan Traditional Chief Peter John, I organized the first Midnight Sun Intertribal Powwow in the Athabaskan land of Fairbanks, Alaska. Our mission was "to bring together Alaska Natives, American Indians, and First Nations Peoples of Canada, in a powwow setting, to share similarities and diversities; to honor the elders and children; and to educate the general public of the heritage and culture of the Indigenous people of North America".

I have had the honor of leading talking circles, conducting weddings, naming ceremonies, and celebrations of life; and have participated in various speaking engagements. I have been blessed by many teachers and mentors along the way, helping me to grasp the deeply spiritual understanding of God and Creation and my fellow man, as I travel the Red Road. I feel like I am finally living into who Creator God made me, and indeed have found "the missing piece" of my identity.

UNEXPECTED MESSENGERS

"All things are the works of the Great Spirit. We should know that He is within all things: the trees, the grasses, the rivers, the mountains, and all the four-legged animals, and the winged peoples; and even more important, we should understand that He is also above all these things and peoples."

Black Elk, Oglala Sioux, 1863-1950

"The Son is the image of the invisible God, the firstborn over all creation. For in him all things were created: things in heaven and on earth, visible and invisible, all things have been created through Him and for Him. He is before all things, and in Him all things hold together."

Colossians 1:15-17

"Are you ready?" he asked.

"I believe I am."

Preparations had been ongoing for a period of time, but today was the day. I hopped into my Native friend's SUV and enjoyed the warmth of the sun streaming in on this late summer day, as he drove to our first stop on the journey. We engaged in light conversation, as we shared our excitement and anticipation, related to the purpose of this trip. We reflected on the gifts Creator God has provided to our peoples and thanked him for this land we get to call home and for the hospitality we receive from the host people of this land, our Athabascan brothers and sisters.

Our purpose this day was in preparation for the cultural/spiritual gathering and celebration to be held the following year. We prayed that Creator would guide us along our journey and provide all that was needed, according to his will.

We arrived at our first "looking place". Tall stony bluffs, dotted with greenery, stood guard over the swirling river below. Yes, this is where we would find what we hoped for, to gift the many guests from the lower forty-eight, Canada, and beyond, who were anticipated to attend the cultural celebration that following year.

We stopped in silence to take in the majesty of the scene before us, smiled at each other knowingly, offered a prayer and began to ascend the bluff. Our prayers were answered bountifully! Large patches of Alaska Gray Sage greeted us, just as we had hoped!

First Nations people have used varieties of this medicinal plant across Turtle Island (North America), for gifting, cleansing, and prayer. Here in Interior Alaska is where the species of Gray Sage flourishes.

This was my first time looking for and gathering this herb, though my partner had plenty of experience. He taught me where, and how, it grows. He showed me how to use the small sharp pruning shears we brought, being careful to only get a few sprigs from each plant, to preserve the plant itself. Then he stepped away, and we worked together in silence. Every now and then we would stop and look across the wide valley to the Alaska Range, towards the south. We were both bound in silent reverence as we beheld the beautiful scene. Our harvest was abundant. My heart swelled with gratitude.

The sudden call of the raven spoke into the silence, causing me to look skyward. Two sets of ravens gracefully glided towards each other above. I love watching our winged relatives! It was mesmerizing watching these two pairs soar towards each other in what seemed like a collision course. Then, as if on divine cue, they each separated and individually flew in the four directions East, South, West, and North. We watched until they were out of sight. My friend and I looked at each other in amazement, with tears of joy brimming in our eyes. We had prayed for guidance! We sensed this was our message that our harvest at this location was complete and done in a good way; and it was time to look for the next spot. So off we went to the next spot for gathering sage. We stopped and picked at several locations down the road, along the river. The sage sprig cuts now nearly filled the back of his SUV.

By then, we were both hungry. We found a roadhouse along the way, had lunch and reflected on how blessed we felt. We discussed how the sage would still need to be hung to dry for a month or two, then sprigs tied together into bundles for gifting.

After lunch, we decided that we would make one or two more stops for sage, and then be done for the day. As we drove for a spell, heading for the next set of bluffs on the river, an eagle swooped down in front of our moving vehicle, and soared off.

We looked at each other, again in amazement, and both spoke the same words to each other at the same time, "We are done!". We shared a joyful laugh. I felt a sense of gratitude, and contentment. Everything was just as it should be, thanks to Creator and his unexpected messengers!

CHAPTER TWO

EMOTIONAL (The Heart)

"That which brings about any intense state of feeling"

(3)

"NEVER BELONGING"

"The more we become willing to depend on a Higher Power, the more independent we are. Therefore dependence, is really a means of gaining true independence of the spirit."

Twelve and Twelve, page 36

"What seemed at first a flimsy reed, has proven to be the loving and powerful hand of God. A new life has been given us or, if you prefer, 'a design for a living' that really works."

Big Book, page 28

"Mom, what does homely mean?"

I was just a child when a relative of the family referred to me in this way. Mom's response to my inquiry went by the wayside, but I will never forget that judgment of me once I learned the meaning of the word.

I was born nine months after my brother Skippy crossed over. He was only fifteen months old. I was Mom and Dad's second child, now the eldest. My older brother had numerous medical maladies from his birth to his passing. I became their special child, and they loved me, but they had one concern. I was tiny. They took me to doctors to see if there was something wrong with me. The medical consensus was that I would just always be small in stature. (By the way, I grew to be 6'4"). During my childhood years, I always felt weak and awkward and was overly sensitive and threatened by everything. This taproot of fear stunted my emotional growth, and I remained selfish and self-centered, craving attention, and seeking acceptance, by acting out and misbehaving. This would, instead, generate further rejection. My only outlet for this emotional pain during those young years was to break down and cry. I was dubbed "crybaby" by my classmates. I was humiliated. I became more withdrawn, alternating with acting out, and saying things I would later regret. I just could not fit in.

I developed an interest in playing hockey and discovered it was the one thing at which I excelled. At age twelve, due to certain zoning rules, I was denied the opportunity to play hockey in my local district. Distrust and rage welled up inside me, against ALL authority figures, from this time on.

I began lying, cheating, and whatever I could do to defy authority, caring nothing about the consequences. By the time I reached junior high school, I started growing in stature. If I perceived a threat, from an authority figure, or a classmate, a switch would flip within me, with no warning, and I would fly into a rage, followed by remorse. This cycle seemed endless. It followed me into adulthood, and for decades thereafter. It was like I lacked control of my emotions. It brought me isolation, and a tough "I don't give a rip! I'll show you!" exterior, while inside, I was still craving attention... this dichotomy became the norm for me.

The only time I felt relief from all this emotional pain was when I drank alcohol. Since age four, when a visiting relative gave me my first drink of alcohol, I liked the way it made me feel. It gave me a false sense of confidence, a mask that I could hide behind. As time marched on, I craved alcohol more and more, securing any kind of booze, anyway I could. This became an obsession for much of my life.

Drowning my emotions in alcohol took its toll on me in every way. I was hopeless, helpless, lost in confusion, lacking the ability to distinguish between right and wrong, good or bad, unable to form healthy relationships and experience the love and acceptance I so craved since childhood.

Then came that day when I came to the end of myself, and surrendered control of my life (or lack thereof), and uttered those four words, "God, please help me!" As the fog started to lift, a new reality began to emerge. Emotions that had been buried were now coming to the surface. There was so much I could not understand about this roller coaster of emotions...gratitude, guilt, remorse, moments of serenity, self-loathing, but most of all hope.

One day, after I had been sober for several months, I was driving the usual 25 miles from town to home. I navigated around a slight bend in the road that I had driven around hundreds of times before. Suddenly, for the first time ever, I beheld all the brilliant and varied shades of green of the trees on the hillsides... the birch, spruce, alder, cottonwood, and willow trees, and even of the grasses along the roadside. Wow! I had never seen this before! It dawned on me at that moment, that I had lived my entire life in shades of gray, without even realizing what I was missing. Tears came to my eyes, as I was overwhelmed by this experience. These were tears of gratitude, wonder, and joy.

I couldn't wait to arrive home to share this wonderment. I called my friend Bill and exclaimed what I had just witnessed. I will never forget his gentle response, "The colors have always been there. Now you are beginning to see! Your emotions are awakening to the beauty of creation. This is a gift." And there were many more gifts to come.

In my pursuit of spiritual, emotional, mental, and physical healing, I discovered that I had been functioning emotionally much like a toddler. In my sobriety, I began to grow into emotional maturity, and I started to experience the love and acceptance that I had craved for all those years, as I enthusiastically did whatever was required to grow into the person who God made me to be. It took time, and a lot of work within my sobriety journey, the Jesus Way, and in my Native walk, to get to where my emotional cup is not only full, but overflowing, to where I have many loving relationships.... with my wife of 35 years, my family, innumerable friends, and most importantly, my loving Creator. My heart is healed.

"For You created my innermost being, you knit me together in my mother's womb. I praise you because I am fearfully and wonderfully made, your works are wonderful, I know that full well."

Psalm 139:13-14

THE ABYSS

"The people walking in darkness have seen a Great Light, on those living in the land of deep darkness a Light has dawned"

Isaiah 9:2

"I cannot take it anymore! I cannot go on living like this. This pain in my back and legs is too much. I'm useless, I can't accomplish anything with this constant pain. It's ruining my life. God, why are you allowing this to happen to me? I pray, I read spiritual books, work with others, and write, seeking answers. God, are you there? Is all this pain real or is it all in my head? I feel ashamed having to ask for pain medicine."

No one, doctors nor any clinicians, seem to have a solution or cure. They do the best they can. I take the prescribed medicine. It helps me some, but the torment of the pain overcomes. I have a love-hate relationship with these medicines, because of their side effects. I endure more MRIs, CAT scans, and tests of all sorts. I try to be active, only to be shot down by this stabbing pain. I hold pity parties that no one shows up to but me. Living has become too difficult. I pray at night that God will take me home. Then in the morning I wake up with a shred of hope, and pray to God for guidance and direction, and perhaps some relief for that day. But alas, by evening, an entire day of pain once again drives me to ask God to take me home. This pattern continues over and over.

My wife watches me deteriorate into the abyss of hopelessness. All my energy is devoted to trying to deal with the pain. I have no energy left for relationship. I put up thick walls that block communication. My silent scowl keeps her at a distance. At times she tries to draw me out, but I shut her down with my negativism. I cannot tell her that I want out of this life, so I live in my self-imposed cocoon. My head keeps swirling with visions of possible means I can use to end my life and have no more pain!

Then one day my wife and I have a real conversation where I reveal to her my suicidal plans. She convinces me to seek help and assures me that we will do this together. She makes some calls which result in an appointment with a physician specializing in helping someone like me.

During our first appointment his first statement validated my struggle. "Enough is enough; your problem is uncontrolled pain. It is in your back, and not in your head.... you are suffering from significant depression because of this physical pain."

He prescribed a new regimen to limit the pain to manageable proportions, to where I gradually began to enjoy life again. This would last a number of years, until the next unexpected turn of events. This would not be my last bout of pain-mediated depression.

CARRYING A GRUDGE

"Marriage among my people was like traveling in a canoe. The man sat in the front and paddled the canoe. The woman sat in the stern, but she steered."

Anonymous (from "365 Days of Walking the Red Road")

"Do not let the sun go down while you are still angry."

Ephesians 4:26

"You are being passive-aggressive," she said to me.

"What is she talking about?"

Our newlywed "pink cloud" had dissipated, and we discovered we did not know how to communicate.

Certain of my broken ways, character flaws, "missing the mark," were removed quickly by the Spirit, such as my constant use of foul language, at the time of my prayer of desperation. Other defects remained for me to work on. I was just learning how to live in sobriety, dealing with a whole lifetime of repressed, buried, and warped emotions. Looking back, now, I realize I was still a child emotionally. My wife will tell you that she was also emotionally immature, related to some of her life experiences. Together, we were a recipe for failure, but Creator had other ideas. We stayed together through much relational adversity because we believed Creator wanted us together, and things of value are worth working for.

I was blessed to have a happily married, sober couple as two of my mentors. One of the tough lessons they taught me was to look at "my side of the street," in any disagreement. I had to begin to face and feel what was going on in me emotionally, and sort through the true and false old beliefs about...well, about everything. My old way was to instantly look "across the street" to blame others, circumstances, inanimate objects, whatever or whoever was handy, for all my failings. And usually, my wife was handy.

Contention ruled our relationship. I expected her to know how I felt. Didn't she understand that I knew the best way to do things? Notice there was no "we", it was all about me, mine, I.

On a beautiful sunny spring day in our first year of marriage, my wife and I began raking our yard together. I observed that she was not thatching out the old grass thoroughly enough. I believed it was my duty to help her out and show her how to rake properly. I walked over to her and took the rake out of her hands and proceeded to demonstrate for her the proper way to accomplish this task.

She looked at me with dismay, and when I handed her the rake back for her to practice this new skill, she took the rake, threw it to the ground, and walked away...for a two-year hiatus from raking the lawn. The next time she picked up a rake and began raking, she had seen the emotional growth in me. She raked the way she wanted to, and I raked the way I wanted to, and it all got done.

As I progressed in my new sober way of living, grew in my relationship with Jesus, and embraced my Native American culture, with its inherent closeness to Creator and creation, my fickle finger of blame slowly started to lose its power. It had kept me wallowing in self-pity, with its associated sulking and silent scorn, and constantly hauling around various grudges, but now I no longer desired to reside there. I turned to prayer, which led me to a place in my studies that held a solution. The dictionary has been a valuable tool in helping me to realize that my definition of things might be a bit off-target. The dictionary definition of scorn is "extreme and open contempt, due to one's opinion of the meanness or unworthiness of an object or person; also, to act or feel toward with disdain." Disdain is "an attitude of superiority." (4) Wow! All that described me.

My wife and I could live in the same house and barely say a word for days, as we built up our walls of offense/defense against each other. My sober-couple mentors helped greatly here. The wife shared that women like to be touched respectfully. My wife and I used to hold hands while driving on our long trips to town when we were newlyweds but that had not happened in a long time. I had to swallow my pride and trust her suggestion. During our next trip to town, I reached out and gently touched my wife's hand with my fingers. She curled her fingers around mine, and we connected. We connected! Something we had not done in a long time.

"Are you criticizing God's handiwork?" the husband of this couple asked in response to my diatribe of my wife's communication deficits. This stopped me in my tracks. Another time, he told me that when I had had enough self-induced pain from emotionally distancing my wife with my critical spirit, I might try listening and seeking to understand her instead.

"Sit down with your wife and say, 'Good or bad, right, or wrong, this is how I feel,' then shut your mouth and let her speak. Do not refute her feelings and see what happens."

This was not easy, but paid dividends the first time I tried it. It removed the judgmental, contentious component of whatever feeling I was about to share. My wife let her guard down and spoke her true feelings, and we had an honest healthy relationship-building conversation. It has since become a valuable tool in our partnership.

I am grateful for the wisdom Creator has sent my way through people like this couple. My wife and I used to say we wished we could have a marriage like theirs. Now, we have become one of those couples that we were so envious of during our first years of marriage.

Meanwhile, I am still trying to grasp what passive-aggressive means, but my wife has not mentioned it in a long time;).

> *"It is a spiritual axiom that every time we are disturbed, no matter what's the cause, there is something wrong with us."*
>
> Twelve and Twelve, page 90

> *"When you arise in the morning, give thanks for the morning light, for your life and strength. Give thanks for your food and the joy of living. If you see no reason for giving thanks, the fault lies in yourself."*
>
> Tecumseh, Shawnee 1768-1813

ALL YOUR FAULT

(a story by Don Standing Bear's wife, Edie Winter Song)

> *"Gideon said to God, "'If You will save Israel by my hand as You have promised- look, I will place a wool fleece on the threshing floor. If there is dew, only on the fleece, and all the ground is dry, then I will know that You will save Israel by my hand as You said. And that is what happened. Gideon rose early the next day; he squeezed the fleece and wrung out the dew- a bowl full of water."*
>
> Judges 6:33-40

He was tall, handsome, gentle, considerate, romantic, and didn't drink alcohol! We talked of God, Alaska, the great outdoors, animals. When he asked me to marry him, of course I said yes. He had to be a gift from God. Just months before we met, we each had a life changing spiritual awakening where we had turned our lives over to the care of God. Now He had put us together.

I believed this, until.... during my last visit to Don in Alaska, before our wedding, he was a different person. He was Race Marshall for the "Granddaddy of them all" the Open North American Championship Sled Dog Race in Fairbanks, Alaska. I had been the center of his attention until then. Now the dog race was, and he was grumpy with me.

I asked him which person was really him, "because I don't want to marry this one."

He replied, "I don't care; do what you want."

I was mortified and cried, then turned to God in prayer. Because this was such a big decision, I asked God for a sign. I had lost my gold dove necklace days earlier. I knelt beside the bed and asked God, "If You want me to marry Don, help me to find the necklace, and if not, don't let me find it, In Jesus name, Amen." I pulled the covers down to get into bed, and there in front of me was the gold dove necklace. So, I married Don.

I was twenty-seven and this would be my second marriage (first husband drank too much alcohol), and I was such a people pleaser, I thought I could have a good relationship with anyone who didn't drink too much alcohol, but this belief was about to be challenged. After we were married, I was still Don's center of attention for a while, and he spoiled me, but that didn't last. I discovered that he had two personalities. The one I knew and loved, and the critical, controlling one, like my ex-husband's.

I had been bullied as a child, and my solution to conflict was always to run away, whether physically or emotionally. I would not stick up for myself, and due to my low self-esteem, I would start believing the lies people told me about myself. When I was 6 years old, my bully told me that I was ugly, and I should have been a boy (my parents dressed me in boys' clothes, but I didn't make that connection at the time). I internalized this and in adulthood, though people told me I looked like a model, I believed I was fooling them; I was still ugly underneath.

I always did well in school and was on the honor roll, but I believed it when my newlywed husband insinuated I was stupid by saying, "Dooyyy" in a derogatory tone anytime I made a mistake. So, I would scowl and clam up and carry my grudge around. If anything went wrong, I would look for some way to make it not my fault, to avoid the criticism. This encouraged me to remain a powerless victim. If anything went wrong around the house, we each would automatically try to blame it on the other. We had some similar maladaptive behaviors.

I am a high energy person, but when my new husband would pout because I did not do all the tasks he expected me to do (I was working full time nights and he and I were training and racing 38 sled dogs, plus I cooked and cleaned), I believed I was lazy. I would still be angry at him for pointing it out, so again, I would clam up, avoid him, and carry my grudge around.

I would also let Don make my decisions for me. Even if I disagreed, I trusted his judgement over my own, and/or I did not want to suffer his silent scorn if I didn't do what he said. If anyone criticized "my" decision, I would point them to Don, because it was his fault. I recalled that my mom, who was nineteen when she married my fifty-two-year-old Dad, did whatever he said, as did we kids. We were never allowed to think for ourselves, and suddenly we were adults, and had never learned that skill. It made sense that I would take up with someone who, like my dad, would think for me. (My dad was loving and encouraging, just too protective).

Don's and my marriage consisted of one big resentment against each other, kept alive by adding little ones along the way to fuel it.

But God had a better plan. I am thankful that He saw fit to send us each the spiritual advisors we needed to help us.

I had no idea how emotionally immature I was until my mentor had me examine my past and mentioned that we can stop growing emotionally due to a traumatic event occurring at a certain age. Mine was my bully. I had no friends because of her. I was an outcast. My 6-year-old needs were never met. So, I was 6 years old emotionally when I married Don, and I was acting like it! I was trapped between people-pleasing my husband and my friends because I so desperately needed to be accepted by everyone! I could not disagree with anyone or make a mistake, because they might not like me. So, I was a people-pleasing perfectionist wimp! Who was I? Whoever you wanted me to be. I was a chameleon.

I learned that the solution to my wimpiness was spiritual in nature. I, like Don, had some defects of character removed when I prayed a similar prayer of relinquishing "control" of my messed-up life to God, but had plenty of broken ways left to work on over time. I had a faith in God, but based on my behavior, I discovered I had more faith in people. They were my "god," because I would do what they said, instead of what the true God (often revealed by my "gut feeling") said. I went against what I knew was right, and this was the root cause of my anger. Really it was anger at myself and my powerlessness, directed outwardly at them. I realized that even my concept of God was based on what my sister told me, and that I had never really sought to learn of God myself. I realized that was what I needed to do. My mentor guided me along as I read, wrote, prayed, and meditated. I had to let go of my preconceived concept and allow God to reveal Himself to me, one on one. Then I had to trust Him to give me courage and protect me when I made decisions that reflected my God-given values, that others disagreed with.

I learned that whenever I became angry, one of my boundaries was being threatened, and I needed to choose a course of action to defend it. I needed to stick up for myself, a new thing for me. When I did that, I discovered, to my amazement, that it brought me peace, instead of fear or anger, regardless of the reaction of others. I learned how to respectfully state my truth, and act on it, without blaming, acquiescing, or reacting to negative feedback.

My first big God-dependent decision that I acted on, was telling my husband that it was important to me to go to church. He did the power pout, but I was not angry at him, or me! I was joyful and experienced a newfound freedom! He could no longer control me with his attitudes! I went to church. He later made amends for trying to get between me and my God.

Shortly thereafter, for the first time ever, I told Don in a calm manner that I was angry at a certain thing he did, and that I would appreciate it if he would not do that thing again. He agreed not to. Again, I spoke my truth respectfully, and he acted respectfully in return.

When he said, "Dooyy!" the next time I made a mistake, I told him that it was hurtful to me and asked that he not do it.

He said, "Okay, I didn't realize it bothered you that much." He never did it again.

Don is neat and organized, but one thing that irked me was finding the knife he used to make peanut butter and jelly sandwiches adhered to the counter with the dried jam "glue." I mentioned it to him, but he would sometimes still leave it there. My mentor advised that I could choose to mention it again (but over three times is nagging); leave it stuck to the counter, and not allow it to bother me; or cheerfully clean it up so I could enjoy a clean counter. Since he did not do it much anymore, I cheerfully cleaned it up, while appreciating his overall neatness.

I had begun on the journey of a faith that worked. I learned to trust my gut feeling and to pray when unsure and consult a trusted spiritual friend when needed. Along with this came the beginnings of emotional maturity; and because Don was traveling his own journey to spiritual and emotional maturity, the beginnings of the happy marriage we have today started to blossom. It really wasn't "all his fault". It was God's idea all along.

MY FATHER'S EYES

"My son, if your heart is wise, then my heart will be glad; indeed, my inmost being will rejoice when your lips speak what is right."

Psalm 23:15-16

THE FIRE

My dad, Andre Grey Wolf, did not answer the phone; unusual for him.

"He must be chatting with one of his friends; I'll try again later," I told my wife Edie, who happened to be visiting me in Arizona, my winter home at the time.

Dad, who lived in Massachusetts, and I routinely talked every morning at this time. Whenever Edie was with me, she joined in on the telephonic visit. She loved Dad and enjoyed spending time with him, also. Each morning, Dad and I would take turns reading aloud from the "Our Daily Bread" daily devotional, (5) and then alternate leading our prayers for the day. We would share our experiences, stories, and dreams, and just generally enjoy our time together. This experience was one that we looked forward to each day, one we rarely missed.

As I was about to call Dad again, the phone rang. I answered, only to hear my sister Chere's panicked voice blurt out, "Dad's house is on fire, and he was rushed to the hospital!"

"What happened," I asked, "Is he okay?"

"I don't know; Heidi (my other sister) and I are on our way there now."

Edie and I sat dumbfounded, not knowing what to do. There we were miles away from our family.

Even in our fog of numbness, we both said, "Let's pray," and we held each other's hands and prayed earnestly for Dad.

Sometimes the answer is not what we desire. Minutes later, the phone rang again. The doctor's voice on the other end sounded somber, "I'm sorry to have to tell you that your dad was pronounced dead on arrival. He had burns on his arms like he was trying to put the fire out, but he had dragged himself away from the flames to the back door before he succumbed to smoke inhalation." (We later found out it was an old faulty electrical outlet that had started the fire).

I could hear my two sisters wailing loudly in the background. I was in shock. Our beloved dad had crossed over. I realized then that this fire was raging as I was trying to call him earlier that morning.

I was so grateful that Edie was with me. Out of the six winter months I spent in Arizona, she took time off work and visited a couple of times. We thanked God that this was during one of them.

As the reality of Dad's death sunk in, we shifted into action. We needed to get back East and be with and help our family. Arrangements had to be made. Things needed to get done. We flew back as soon as we could.

As the oldest living son of Mom (Esther Night Dancer, also recently deceased) and Dad, the responsibility of the patriarch was now passed on to me. I leaned into Jesus for the comfort and strength I needed, so I could be there to comfort my family and our many family friends.

As our family began preparing for Dad's "Celebration of Life," two weeks after his passing, I began to reflect on my relationship with him, and how influential he was in my life.

IS GOD LIKE MY DAD?

As I learned in a spiritual retreat a few years prior, dads play such a key role in the lives of their kids, that...even our concept of God and relationship with Him, at least initially, tends to be like our relationship with our birth father. This can be an asset or an obstacle to overcome, when developing a relationship with our Heavenly Father, depending on our earthly father's character.

At this retreat, I had witnessed a variety of reactions to this revelation. Some there had horrific childhoods and were antagonistic towards this discussion, but eventually were willing to look at the correlation. Then the chaplain shared this simple but enlightening exercise, which was a turning point for many of the men there.

I now encourage you, the reader, to get a piece of paper and pen and doing this exercise yourself. Do one step at a time. Do not read ahead to the next step until you complete the step prior. You will see why at the end of it. Here is the exercise:

Step 1: Take a piece of blank writing paper and fold it in half vertically. On the left half, list all the things a dad should NOT be, ex. absent, punitive, critical.

Step 2: Then on the right half of the paper, list all the characteristics of what a dad SHOULD be, ex, loving, supportive, present.

Step 3: Tear the paper in half vertically down the middle and throw the left half away.

Step 4: Review the remaining list.

You now have in your hand, an accurate description of your Heavenly Father. He has put that desire for this kind of Father in each of us, because this Father is Him, and He loves you and wants a relationship with you.

Bask in this for a moment.

Now, about our imperfect earthly fathers...we expect them to be perfect, like our Heavenly Father, but they can't be. We don't know what they have experienced in their lives that influenced them to become as they are. Hurt people hurt people.

Once we know the love of our Heavenly Father, that hole in the soul starts to be filled, and we can take the pressure off our earthly fathers.

This exercise led some of the men there to seek to understand and even forgive their fathers. Some could speak this forgiveness to their fathers personally. Others had to do so over their father's gravesite. Even those whose fathers were still "undeserving," were able to relieve themselves of that pain and negative energy which influenced their daily lives, by learning "forgiveness, the gift you give yourself" when you extend it to others.

MY DAD

In my life experience, I was the thoughtless, self-centered, undeserving one, not my dad.

While growing up, I always wanted to be around my dad. We would go places together, but we seldom talked. If we did, it was usually about sports. His dad was a drunk and my dad had no real father figure to model after, so he did not know how to communicate with me. During my childhood and youth, my dad worked full-time as a milkman. He also had a number of part-time jobs that required him to be away from home for many hours, or even full days at a time. I always asked to go along just to be around him, and he would take me whenever he could. Strange as it may seem, however, I had an unhealthy fear of my dad, really for no reason I can think of... much like my relationship with God at that time, perhaps because I lived in fear in general. My dad was the disciplinarian in the family, but he always did it with my best interests in mind. He had a booming voice and when I behaved badly, he got my attention quickly and I respected him. He was active in various volunteer positions, drum corps, basketball, hockey....and was loved and esteemed by the community, and by any who knew him. I know I caused him and Mom much heartache and grief, though they were also spared the worst of it by my move to Alaska.

LOVE LETTER FROM MY DAD

I remembered how, years ago, at the age of thirty-two, and after I uttered that life-altering prayer, "God help me!" This tough Alaskan man worked up the nerve to call my dad and tell him that I was finally seeking a solution to my problem of alcoholism. I was afraid of how he would react.

My dad's voice on the other end of the phone line was so full of compassion and support, that it began to diminish the shame, guilt and remorse that plagued me. He gave me the gift of forgiveness and hope, not unlike that given me by my Heavenly Father in answer to my desperate prayer. Dad had known I was in trouble, even though, for many years, I lived five thousand miles away. Six years prior to that phone call, Dad wrote me a letter that I still have today. Below are excerpts from this letter:

"It has been a long time since I've taken the time to sit down and write you a letter...I realize you have had a bad year in many ways... I wish that I could be up there with you, even if it were only for moral support.

I do miss you very much. I hope you realize that as a father and son relationship I don't think that two guys were as close to each other as we were in our activities. We went to many places together as a family... We spent many hours together. In all those years, I don't think you ever saw me drunk, so you're drinking doesn't come from home.

In reading your letter again, I am wondering if we are taking your drinking too seriously, or do you think it's getting to be a problem where you should try to get some help from a social worker or even AA?

I am glancing back at your letter again; you mention that the only time you were happy is when you drink...

I know I was never much for writing letters, but the point I am trying to get to you is that I love you and miss you very much, and when you have problems, I feel them almost as much as you do, because you are still very much a part of me.

Just stay strong and I'm sure that things will get better, because they can't get any worse.

This summer I plan to send Mom up to see you, even if I have to remortgage the house. That's all she talks about. Maybe when I reach fifty-five, I will take early retirement and sell out and move up to Alaska.

I'm having a hard time keeping my eyes open,

Miss you, Love, Dad"

I had no idea Dad felt this way. I had been wrapped up in my own little world of self-imposed insanity from a bottle. I had believed that Dad was ashamed of me. Unbeknownst to me he was there all along with an unquenchable, unfathomable, sacrificial love, reminiscent of my Heavenly Father's love.

"...for deep down in every man, woman, and child, is the fundamental idea of God. It may be obscured by calamity, by pomp, by worship of other things, but in some form or other, it is there." (6)

Early in my "new life", I realized God had also always been there, though I did not know or see Him then. He even listened to those "Get me out of this one and I'll never do it again!" prayers, knowing all along

I couldn't keep these promises. I was an egomaniac with an inferiority complex. I was a mess, but unbeknownst to me, He loved me anyway, even then, just as did my earthly dad.

Even in this new life I didn't know how to begin to talk to God. I figured He was ashamed of me, too. However, He welcomed this prodigal son, as I struggled to reach out to Him with my simple prayer of "Please" (I didn't know what else to say then) in the mornings, and "Thank You" in the evenings.

God led me to a fellowship of sober men and women, who became my teachers, encouragers, and examples in this new life. They came from all backgrounds, young, elders, professionals, blue collar workers, clergy, believers, atheists, agnostics, rich and poor. Over the next many years, I did the footwork they told me I needed to do to stay sober and become "happy, joyous, and free."

I learned to talk to God about anything, and to listen for His "voice" in the many ways which He communicates to us. As I grew closer to God, I grew closer to my dad, too. We became best of friends, staying connected by phone and in person. As we parted ways, or ended phone calls, we would close with,

"I love you, Dad;"

"I love you, Son."

At age thirty-eight, I was set to graduate with two degrees. I said to my wife, "What a joy it would be if Dad could be here." She agreed with a sigh of disappointment that he could not be present. The day of commencement, Edie and I stopped to pick up my youngest sister, Lynn, who lived in Fairbanks. Her front door opened, but it was not Lynn who appeared first. It was Dad! Edie, Lynn, and our friends had kept this secret so well. What a joy! Dad beamed as he posed with me for my post-graduation pictures, and so did I! Dad told me how proud he was of me. How many sons wish they could hear their dad say that! It was a joyous and unforgettable experience!

THE SECRET

As kids, my sister Chere and I would visit Dad's mom, "Meme," as we called her. She secretly educated us in the way of our Native American ancestors, but in those days, it was not cool to be Native, so she charged us not to tell anyone, and we honored her request. My dad didn't talk about it. Only Meme did. I didn't think too much about it.

Then in 1990, while attending the University of Alaska, Fairbanks, I collaborated with my Criminal Justice professors to do a research project on Native Lands and jurisdiction. My immersion in researching this subject begin to awaken those old memories of what Meme had told us. I began to feel drawn towards things Native. Then, the memory of hearing that drumbeat those years ago, during the Festival of Native Arts at the University, sealed it. I had to know more about this part of my identity. Finally, I called Dad. As chance (God) would have it, Dad had been wondering the same thing. Meme had crossed over many years prior, so we could no longer avail ourselves of her knowledge. So, while I was busy doing my research at the University, Dad searched out our Native genealogy.

Dad and Mom began attending local powwows in Massachusetts where they lived, and over time, my dad became the "elder" for our tribal council. I went back East for powwows, gatherings, and council meetings. As the guest from Alaska, I was asked to open each meeting and gathering with prayer. Mom, Dad, my sisters (Chere, Heidi, and Lynn) and I would spend many such happy occasions together at these events. Even my nieces and nephews got involved.

Meanwhile in Fairbanks, Alaska, where I lived, I joined the "Walking Hawk" Intertribal Native American powwow drum group, and became one of the lead singers, and eventually became drum keeper of another powwow drum, "Walks the Nations", which I used to teach elementary school children about the drum, dance, and Native culture.

Meme would not have minded her secret getting out. I think she would have been happy.

As I embraced my Native heritage, in addition to the Jesus Way, and my sobriety fellowship, I felt like I was growing into the identity of who God made me to be. As I read more of God's Word, I learned that God was bigger than the "box" we so often try to put Him in. Dad, too, was growing spiritually. Each of us were both student and teacher. We felt like our purpose was to assist others in their healing from broken ways. Dad had his physical challenges. He was diagnosed with diabetes in his forties and started on pills for it. He immediately changed his diet accordingly. He had such self-discipline. Later he still had to transition to injectable insulin. Then he had to have open heart surgery. I flew back East for that. I helped Mom tend to his recovery. I helped him shower, and dress. He watched me tie his shoes one day and said, "I used to do that for you until you learned to do it yourself." I reminded him of how he flew to Alaska to do the same for me after my back surgery in 1984, plus take care of my kennel of sled dogs. Our eyes met and we both smiled.

Dad and I loved to sing and dance our prayers at the powwows. He had a strong but humble spirit about him. People would listen to him and seek his counsel. One day as I sat with him, after a number of "brothers and sisters" met with him, he leaned over to me and said,

"Why are these people doing this?"

I replied, "Dad, they love you and respect you, and know how valuable you are to them." Then he turned and greeted the next person.

Despite Dad's self-discipline, the diabetes caught up with him. His foot had become infected and caused sepsis, leading to confusion. He was scheduled for surgery. When we flew back East, we met our family at the hospital. Dad did not recognize us. As he was taken off to surgery, we were told that he may not survive the procedure. But after a time, the surgeon came and told us that he was in recovery, and we could go see him. I reached out to Dad's hand. He clasped mine. His eyes opened and he said, "Good to see you, Son. Did they take it off?"

I responded, "Yes."

He sighed and said, "Don't leave."

Eventually, despite having his lower left leg amputated, Dad ended up learning to walk and dance at powwows with a prosthesis and cane.

My last visit with Dad, which I did not know was to be our last visit until we meet again in Heaven, had a surreal feel to it. I have since realized that I was ofttimes "in the Spirit." Mom had crossed over several years prior to this visit, so it was just Dad and me. He expressed how much he missed Mom and I agreed. We would go for drives and visit family. We spent much quality time together. We went to the farm where Mom grew up; we drove up the old dirt road where they courted; and we went to Mount Wachusett, a special place for them and for our family as we were growing up.

I just studied Dad, watched his eyes, facial expressions, mannerisms, and listened closely to his voice when he spoke. It didn't matter if we were having a meal in front of the TV, watching a movie, or were at our weekly tribal council meetings. God knew I would need these special memories, because the fire would soon take my beloved Dad from us.

CELEBRATION OF A SPECIAL LIFE

Prior to Dad's Crossing over ceremony, my sisters, nieces, nephews, and my "warrior" (bodyguard) James Stormhorse, all met at the same restaurant that Dad had taken us all to on our last visit. We all sat down for our family meal at that same table. Dad's seat at the head of the table was assigned to me. That "in the Spirit" sense came over me. As I sat and watched our family eat and interact and share stories, it was as though Dad was there, observing through my eyes. It was powerful but strangely calming, just watching and listening.

Later that evening, the Tribal Hall was packed with family and friends, to honor Andre Grey Wolf. I sat in the circle, again "in the Spirit," watching and listening. Chief Roland requested that I open in prayer, which I was honored to do. My father watched through my eyes and listened in spirit, to a full evening of stories, and tears of grief, from so many, whose lives he had touched.

The big drum had been set up, and was awaiting the first beat, to lead in the Mik'maq honor song, to be followed by the "Traveling Song," which is performed to honor a member who has crossed over.

Chief Roland reserved a seat which faced the East, for me, beside Dad's chair, occupied now only by his drumstick. We sang powerfully. Dad must have enjoyed it.

As our family and friends filtered out of the hall, my nephew Jeremy pointed to the sky. There, shining bright through a thin film of haze, was the January moon, known in Native circles as the Wolf Moon.

MOM

Esther Night Dancer was the youngest daughter of a minister. She called herself "the black sheep of the family." Mom's roots were Dutch. Her mom wanted her to marry someone of her own religion. Instead, she married Andre Grey Wolf. They were high school sweethearts. When their first baby died, her mom told her it was because she married Dad. This was not true, but Mom believed her and turned further away from a God who would do such a thing. We sometimes don't realize the gravity of the words we speak. The Holy Spirit grieved.

Still, Mom shared her love with 68 (not a typo!) foster babies, as well as her own children, from the 1950's to the 1970's. She was also a gifted writer and poet, who loved books about Alaska, and hoped to go there someday. Her dream was realized when my youngest sister Lynn, and I moved to Mom's beloved state, giving occasion for her and Dad, following his retirement, to drive up from Massachusetts nine times, with their cab-over camper, and stay for much of the summers.

Meanwhile, once Dad started getting involved in his Native heritage, Mom was happy to join him. Mom enjoyed participating in the Native American powwows, celebrations, and events. The same God she had turned away from drew her, as she was attracted to living life in the Spirit, as these Native friends did. They lived as Jesus said to live, honoring Creator God first in all things, and loving their neighbors, honoring, and respecting and caring for the elders and children, as well as Creation, and trying to live by the old ways, in the modern world.

Unfortunately, as Mom approached her eighties, she developed Alzheimer's disease, which progressed to where Dad had to be her constant caretaker, unable to leave her alone in the house.

She became increasingly angry at God and Dad. This was a very difficult season for Dad, who was still mentally very sharp, but physically limited. My two sisters who lived close by, would help all they could, but they worked, too. Dad was not sleeping and was getting worn out, when someone suggested an assisted living home for Mom, but Dad said he had promised never to put her in such a place. He would be true to his promise, no matter how hard it was for him. He would call me for prayer and encouragement.

One night my phone rang at 10pm. It was Dad. It was 2am East Coast time. He said, "Mom wants to talk to you."

He had tried to calm her down and reason with her, but she "kept cussing up a storm." He finally gave up. He put Mom on the phone and remained on his extension. She had recently been diagnosed with terminal lung cancer which had spread. The desperation in Mom's voice was evident. She cried as she said,

"Donnie, I want you here! I don't know what's going on. What's wrong with me?"

Edie and I already had tickets to fly back there, but not for another month. I told her, "We are coming soon, Mom."

She kept asking what was wrong with her. I was praying this whole time to be a channel for God's message to Mom. I said,

"Mom, you have cancer, and it's terminal."

She became quiet. I then asked her if I could pray for her. Normally she would have belittled prayer. But this time, her voice calmed down, and she said,

"Yes, please!"

I don't recall the prayer, but as it came to a close, she said to me in a soft, gentle voice,

"Thank you, Donnie."

Then she hung up her phone. Dad, still on the other phone, said,

"Thank you, Son."

Dad and my sisters subsequently reported to me that Mom did not utter another cuss at God, Dad, nor anyone else after that. She even agreed to go to a hospice facility, which she had vehemently refused prior to that call. She transferred there and got the care she needed. Dad stayed at her bedside but was able to finally rest. Mom crossed over peacefully before Edie and I arrived.

> *"For God has not given us the spirit of fear; but of power, and of love, and of a sound mind."*
>
> 2 Timothy 1:7
>
> *"The father of a righteous child has great joy; a man who fathers a wise son rejoices in him. May your father and mother rejoice; may she who gave you birth be joyful."*
>
> Psalm 23:24

CHAPTER THREE

MENTAL (the mind)

Intellectual, of, or pertaining to the mind (thoughts)

(7)

A SECOND CHANCE

"To clothe a man falsely is only to distress his spirit…
". Luther Standing Bear,

Oglala Sioux, 1868-1937

"In our language there is no word to say inferior or superiority or equality because we are all equal."

Alanis Obomsawin, Abenaki

"Did you know your GPA score was 0.07?," the Dean asked me as he thumbed through my college transcripts, "and you were expelled from the University in 1980."

I had no recollection of this fact. I first learned of it at this time, nine years later during an appointment with the Dean of the College, when I applied to return to the University of Alaska. He also revealed that I had amassed 104 credits, but only six were in upper division classes. And my SAT scores were Math: 240, and English: 260. Not too impressive.

From my earliest memories as a three- or four-year-old, I lived in extreme fear, which continued into my adult life, a corroding thread woven into my entire existence. My childhood home was safe. Mom and Dad loved us and were supportive and provided for our needs. Yet this unfounded fear kept me locked in a self-inflicted mental cage. I was shy and withdrawn. All new people, places, and things were unsafe. How does a child grow when everything new is a threat? All my thoughts and dreams, whether while awake or asleep, were destructive. Nightmares were common and repetitive. Many nights I would wake and be screaming that the bogeyman was going to get me. I had a tough time with darkness and bedtime, even into my early thirties. I had to sleep with the light on.

As I entered elementary school, it did not take long for the teachers to realize that I was having trouble learning and retaining the materials of the grade level I was in. Mom helped me a lot by reading to my sisters and me from classic books, but I still had difficulty in comprehending what she read. I was too afraid to ask questions or speak up about my confusion.

By third grade, whenever reading class started, a couple of other students and I were taken out of class to a room with a "special teacher". This was embarrassing and led to being made fun of by a lot of the other students. Now shame and inadequacy compounded my underlying fear and enveloped my whole being.

By the time I reached middle school I had perfected the fine art of cheating. I lacked the confidence to challenge myself to even attempt to learn any subject. Mom really tried to help. She ended up even providing me with answers for my homework problems. My book reports consisted of copying pages from the books I was assigned to read. I did not have the ability to write what I may have thought of on my own. I was paralyzed by fear.

In the eighth and ninth grade my fear began to manifest itself differently. Like a cornered animal, I would lash out in fits of rage at the other male students during or between classes, which landed me in the principal's office on numerous occasions. These fits of rage came with no warning and no on/off switch. They just happened. One of my teachers made statements about my being "stupid and not able to do anything. You are not going to amount to anything." This further fed my festering inadequacy, fear and rage.

By the end of my freshman year in public school, I started really getting out of hand. I had no friends, no allegiance to any of my peers or teachers, and I was tired of getting pulled out of class to spend time with the "special teacher" to the subsequent belittlement by both classmates and teachers. I couldn't take anymore. I threatened one of my teachers. This obviously did not go over well with my parents or the school. I endured the resulting disciplinary actions, but nothing really changed inside, and I was allowed to return to school thereafter.

The only skill I had, other than cheating and lying, was in ice hockey. This skill qualified me to attend a private prep high school. My parents could not afford the full cost of the school, so my grandparents helped to cover the cost. My family tried to help any way they could to keep me in school. My hockey skills blossomed, but my abilities as a student stagnated. If it were not for my outstanding abilities as a hockey player, I would not have made it through prep school. I was so gifted in the game of hockey that during my junior year of high school, a number of colleges and universities were lining up with scholarship offers for me to play hockey for their institutions. They anxiously awaited my SAT scores. Back in the early 1970s much weight was given to these Scholastic Aptitude Test scores for acceptance into colleges, and especially for awarding of scholarships.

I remember the day I attempted to take these SAT's. Anxiety and fear gripped me, and I was incapacitated. I muddled through in my fear induced fog and dreaded hearing the results. I was convinced that I lacked intelligence, and this proved to be a self-fulfilling prophecy.

It turns out that my scores were so low that they thought there must be some mistake. I was encouraged to retake the SAT tests, to see if the scores were indeed indicative of my intellectual capacity. The repeat scores prove no different. All the potential universities and colleges dropped their communications with me as soon as they received these SAT scores.

During my senior year in prep school, my classmates were receiving their acceptance letters to further their education. Being a student in a prep school means exactly that, preparing for college. In the assembly room all the senior students' names were posted in large letters and beside them was listed which school they were accepted into. A couple of classmates opted for military service and that notice was posted as well. Mine was blank.

A couple of days before commencement (yes, I did graduate and was not at the bottom of my class. I was next to last), most unexpectedly, I did receive notice of acceptance to a junior college on a hockey scholarship, and I accepted.

Over the two years at this junior college, I coped with my insecurities by imbibing large amounts of alcohol and further honed the skills of lying, and cheating, and resorted to buying term papers, to survive in academia. Even hockey started to suffer from my copious alcohol intake, but for some reason the school allowed me to graduate, despite my incomplete status and failing grades in some of my classes.

After graduation, fear, inadequacy, and dishonesty continued to control me, leading to dead ends in every aspect of my life. Hockey-drinking, relationships-drinking, drinking-arrests, jobs-drinking, no job-drinking. Due to circumstances that I had brought upon myself, I needed to change where I lived. How about a 5000-mile geographical cure? The only problem was, when I landed in Fairbanks, Alaska on August 25, 1975, fleeing my troubles, the cause of them – me – came along.

The University of Alaska Fairbanks accepted this mess as a student.... perhaps because the Alyeska pipeline was being constructed, and so many young adults were working, making big bucks and the University needed to fill the dorms and classes with students. My ability to function and apply myself to education was, if anything, even worse than before. In order to stay in the dorms on campus so that I had housing and food, I took classes in Physical Education, First Aid, Trapping, and Shooting. To get through the more intellectual classes, I cheated and had others take tests and write papers for me. I became a real user of people.

I was in and out of school over the next several years and held jobs that did not depend on any real mental capacity. When I became unemployable after a back injury in 1983, I continued to do what had become normal, I drank alcohol. This earned me more jail time and even residency in a psych unit for a bit. I had damaged whatever intellect that remained.

Then on April 5, 1986, in my complete brokenness, I asked God to please help me. As soon as I said this prayer, God answered by prompting me to call my friend who had recently found a successful way of living without drinking. He answered the phone and said to come right over, and we spent the afternoon talking. He shared the solution he had found, including a fellowship of others seeking sobriety.

From the moment of that prayer, I had become teachable. What happened to me as the result of that prayer is miraculous. God instilled in me a measure of hope. I became hungry; hungry for life, hungry to learn, eager to understand concepts. This transition from my drunken state of despair into a new life of sobriety was not easy. I still could not read or write. I was functioning (as some of my new teachers revealed to me) at the capacity of a second grader. Plus, it took time for my mind to clear up enough to be able to grasp simple concepts. Fortunately, several different men were willing to become my teachers. They spent hours, days, and weeks with me as I learned to read and write. They encouraged me to speak up when called upon. Most importantly, they inspired me to turn my will and my life over to the God who had answered my prayer of desperation.

The surgeries to correct my back injury had not gone well and kept me in a state of being unemployable. During this time in my new life of becoming teachable, I was encouraged by several mentors, to never stop seeking and searching. I learned that I was indeed capable of learning, and I began to enjoy it! Gradually the desire to pursue a higher education developed, and with it, the courage to apply to the University of Alaska Fairbanks as a student once again.

The Dean listened as I explained the change in my life that made me believe I could succeed in academia this time around. He sensed my maturity and earnestness and recommended I be accepted as a student, but under academic probation. I was indeed accepted, but then I wondered if my capacity to really apply myself to schoolwork would become my reality. I had to battle worry, anxiety, and self-doubt, not to mention the degree of self-discipline that would be necessary to succeed.

One of my mentors came up with what seemed to me a novel idea, "Treat school like a job." I needed to keep it simple. "Be at campus at 8 AM, take a lunch time, when not in class, spend time in the library studying or doing homework assignments. Leave campus at 5 PM. This is your fundamental work week."

This gave me evenings with my wife, and time to continue my life of sobriety. Saturday was my day to take off and have fun. Sunday was a day of rest and some catch-up reading. I not only became teachable, I also miraculously found the ability, through willingness, to become self-disciplined.

That first semester was powerful in awakening in me a new paradigm as a student. I worked with my academic advisers and sought out the professors for clarification on any aspects from class that were not clear to me.

But then came that first exam. It was devastating. I froze up. All the familiar old denizens of unworthiness and self-doubt in my abilities reared their ugly heads. This class was very interactive, and I participated in the classroom discussions. The papers I completed for it received good grades, but I just could not complete the exam. The professor of this class was also my academic advisor. She could sense something was wrong by observing me during the class exam time.

I was devastated as I left the exam room. My old enemies had overcome me, and I had failed. My professor contacted me the next day and asked me to come meet with her, and I agreed. "What happened?" she inquired. "I know you know all this material." "I just froze up," I replied.

She pulled out a clean exam sheet and said, "Let's talk about this." She went through the exam verbally with me and wrote down my answers, and we discussed the details of each question, one at a time. She was encouraging and rekindled the fire of hope in me that, "Yes, indeed, I can do this, I am teachable! " She informed me that I scored a B on the exam! The curse had been broken!

As the semester rolled on, a new confidence blossomed within me, and with anticipation and eagerness I dove in as I prepared for, and took each written exam and wrote each paper, MYSELF!

Grades came out after the semester closed. I had taken sixteen credits resulting in a GPA of 3.85. This time, it was impressive! The desire to learn proved fruitful. I was not stupid after all! In fact, I was on the Dean's list for academic achievement! I continued this learning project and received two degrees from the University of Alaska Fairbanks.

One of the great joys of completing this season of education was when my dad surprised me and flew five thousand miles, up from Massachusetts, to attend my graduation ceremony and celebration. I was elated. He was too.

"Apply your heart to instruction and your ears to words of knowledge."

Proverbs 23:12

METLAKATLA

"The One Above Us All is spirit, and all who honor and serve the Great Spirit must do so in spirit and truth."

John 4:24 FNV

"There is one God looking down on us all. We are all children of one God. God is listening to me. The sun, the darkness, the winds, are all listening to what we now say."

Goyathlay (Geronimo), Apache, 1829-1909

THE PLANK

I stood on the deck watching the cedar plank floating in the water, a few feet offshore. For reasons unbeknownst to me until later, I was mesmerized by its movements. Each tiny ocean wave would bring it closer to the shore, but just as it seemed about to make contact, an undercurrent would bring the plank back out into the ocean. What was the meaning of this? More would be revealed.

DOUG

Doug and I first met during World Eskimo Indian Olympics (WEIO), a four-day event held annually in Fairbanks, Alaska, featuring various traditional Native athletic competitions, drum groups, music, dance, storytelling, and art; where I had a booth selling my artwork. Doug was director of "Young Warriors," a servant team of volunteer young adults who assisted the organizers of the event in numerous capacities. Doug also led "120 Drums", a hand drum worship ministry team which performed at WEIO and invited everyone in attendance to participate.

Doug began spending more time at my booth, and he encouraged me to "keep with the gift." I wasn't quite sure which gift he was referring to, but I certainly enjoyed his visits.

Over the next several years, at the various Native gatherings and shows, Doug and I continued to build our friendship. He had a genuine loving spirit, effortlessly embracing his indigenous roots and his faith in Jesus; serving as a significant role model for me, who was struggling in this area. I soon discovered that Doug also was a friend of Richard Twiss, whose book "One Church, Many Tribes," (8) had been life-changing for my wife and me. We each shared appreciation for Richard's wisdom.

But as helpful as our discussions with Doug were during these visits, I still struggled with reconciling the Western "Christian" religious teachings that had been imposed on me, with the spiritual value of Native ways that I felt so drawn to in my heart. Doug's reassurance that I would find "The Way" gave me some degree of hope. But he could see the uncertainty in my face. "You'll see!" Doug would say.

THE INVITATIONS

Then one day I received a phone call from Richard Twiss, himself, inviting me to attend a gathering called "Wiconi," meaning Living Waters, in the Lakota language. It is an annual Jesus Way gathering/powwow in Oregon. At the time I was living in so much physical pain from my old back injuries that I sorrowfully declined his invitation.

A few seasons later I received a call from Doug, almost insisting that my wife Edie, and I travel with him to Ketchikan and Metlakatla, Alaska.

On the way, we would be joined by his friends Guy and Bill, and meet up with Richard Twiss (none of whom we had met before), in Ketchikan. Doug informed us that we would be taken care of by the host nation, the Tsimshian, while in Metlakatla. While in Ketchikan, a Native family, Norm, and Sonja would be our hosts. Creator gave me a nudge, and we agreed to go, not really knowing why, or what to expect.

"You must be Don Standing Bear!" a cheerful voice proclaimed as we were settling into our seats on the flight out of Fairbanks.

I looked up to see this big warm smile, matched by sparkling eyes. He introduced himself, "Hi, I'm Guy!" We exchanged brief greetings and he continued to find his seat. Our plane stopped in Anchorage to pick up Doug and Bill. Doug saw Edie and me, and just as with Guy, a big smile lit up his face. Bill boarded separately from Doug, so we wouldn't get to meet him until later. "All right, guys! Good to see you!" said Doug, followed by his characteristic giggle of joyfulness.

Despite these warm greetings, however, I remained apprehensive. I had prayed to be teachable, and to be a channel for God to work through me; and I had a hunch that this had something to do with the answer to that prayer. It was as if these guys knew something I didn't, and they relished in this adventure.

Norm and Sonja greeted us all on our arrival to Ketchikan. We finally got to meet Bill...another big smile and heartfelt greeting. We had dinner together and then met Richard at the ferry which would take us to the island of Annette, on which Metlakatla is located. Richard greeted us warmly and treated us as if he had always known us.

Once on the ferry, we were invited up to the pilot house. The captain of the ferry, Steve, lived in Metlakatla, and would be one of the hosts for our entourage. Our five (mostly new) friends talked and laughed with ease, including us in their discourse.

After a long day of travel, we arrived in Metlakatla and were greeted by our hosts and escorted to our appointed residences for our stay.

Richard, Edie, and I stayed at our ferry captain's mother in law's house and got to visit some before turning in for the night.

THE BADGER

Early the next morning, I awakened and walked into the kitchen to pour my first cup of coffee. Richard was already up and working on his laptop computer. We exchanged "good morning" greetings. I sat down in a loveseat looking out a sliding glass door facing the bay. I started sipping my coffee.

Richard allowed me a few sips, then asked,

"Did you hear that badger under the house last night?"

I looked over at him, puzzled. He said, a bit more emphatically,

"I said, 'Did you hear that badger under the house last night?'"

"What are you talking about?" I replied, still mystified.

He responded, "There was a really loud badger under the house last night making all kinds of noise."

Then he continued, "I finally realized it was you, snorting and snoring!"

It was my sleep apnea (I now use CPAP, so no more snoring). That day Edie and I found ourselves placed with a different host for the remainder of our stay.

THE CELEBRATION

The following days were filled with workshops, meetings, and visits with residents. Doug had informed me that we were invited along to observe and experience, and to bring our regalia and my artwork, so we could participate in the evening celebrations at the community center, where I could also display my jewelry to sell.

These evening gatherings turned out to be all-out celebrations!

Hospitality is of paramount importance in Native culture. People gathered and visited as tables were set up and traditional foods prepared. Doug, Bill, and Guy set up the staging for their musical worship performance. They are each recording artists, with flute, drums, and guitar, respectively, but they didn't have opportunity to perform together very often. They began to practice, and their music just flowed. Their camaraderie and laughter brought a smile to my face. The local children were intrigued with the drums, and Bill invited them up to have a firsthand experience with the drum set; more happy faces! Excitement was in the air in anticipation of the evening's festivities.

After the feast and socializing with the locals, the festivities began. Protocol, very important in Native cultures, was followed each evening. Elders were recognized with respect and honor. I made sure to gift several of my pieces to the appropriate elders.

The worship team performed, then Richard spoke and inspired us with stories of worshipping God the way He made us, using the gifts from our culture of origin.

When Richard finished speaking, we had the honor of being a part of the living example of what he had just described. The host tribe of Tsimshian people donned their beautiful, typically red, black, and white regalia, with their blankets (capes) displaying the artful depiction of the clan they belonged to, the four main ones being Eagle, Raven, Killer-Whale, and Wolf. One elder, Peter, had blue on white regalia, with a cross in the center of his blanket, along with the Killer Whale symbol of his clan. Some other dancers had crosses on their regalia, too. We each donned our own traditional regalia, some with ribbon shirts or dresses, some with beaded leather vests.

When all were ready, one of the Tsimshian clan drum groups led opening ceremonies, singing and drumming, as we entered, one by one, dancing to the drumbeat, each in his or her own traditional style, though we also took joy in learning and joining in with the host nation's dance style as the dancing continued, with the drum groups from the remaining clans also performing. The drummers, men and women, would line up in front of the stage and hold their drums up high above their heads, singing and swaying in unison with their strong and joyful voices filling the auditorium. As the evening continued, various individuals or groups would perform honor songs, specials, intertribal songs, or "just for fun" songs.

My spirit was blissful! Here were people celebrating life together in song, dance, and art... many of them Jesus Way people, worshiping Him in the way they knew best, in the beauty of their own culture...in the way He made them! This was what I had been searching for...how to worship Creator God Jesus, in the context of my Native heritage. The two are not mutually exclusive after all! Despite what I had been taught, my heart knew the truth all along. And here it was in front of me! I could sense the presence of the Holy Spirit here. I did not want to leave. The evening eventually came to a close, but it was an experience I would never forget. I was so grateful that Doug had insisted I come.

Another blessing from this trip was the time I got to spend talking with Richard. Unfortunately, he crossed over a few years after this trip. But here, he spoke of how we each have gifts (which are our ministry), and mine was my artwork, and to always give credit to the Giver, Creator God.

On our last evening in Metlakatla, the six of us gathered where Richard was staying, to reflect on our experiences. The stirring that had awakened within me became too much, and I broke down and wept. Each of the men shared their hearts with me...the wonder and the growth they had seen in me. It was as if they knew what I was to experience there, and they wanted to be a part of it. Each shared his personal stories of past conflicts similar to mine, and relevant Bible verses that touched their souls. Edie, too, shared her heart...of the wonder and joy and gravity of the experience. The men laid their hands on both of us and prayed over us. I was humbled and grateful. I was sad that we were to leave the next morning.

THE SHORE

So, there I was, that next morning, watching that cedar plank. There is a book (9) that has helped me in my spiritual journey over the last few decades. On page 53, it says,

"Some of us had already walked far over the Bridge of Reason towards the desired shore of faith. The outlines and the promise of the New Land had brought luster to tired eyes and fresh courage to flagging spirits. Friendly hands had stretched out in welcome. We were grateful that reason had brought us so far. But somehow, we couldn't quite step ashore. Perhaps we had been leaning too heavily on reason that last mile and we did not like to lose our support."

I had difficulty understanding that portion of text until now.

That cedar plank in the ocean that got so close to shore was me. Those friendly hands were those of Doug, Guy, Bill, and Richard. I had been trying to reason my way to the answer to my dilemma, and to understanding God's plan for me. My experience here had allowed the plank to finally dock. It was an epiphany! From now on, I could worship Jesus the way He made me, and use the gifts He had given me, and point people to Him! At last! I experienced shalom, wholeness, and peace with who I am. I couldn't wait to tell my friends!

Doug and Bill were on their way to pick us up to catch the ferry back to the mainland. When they arrived, they were playing 'seventies rock' on the radio loudly. As Edie and I hopped into the back seat, they both looked at us with wide grins. Once seated, I blurted out, "I have something to tell you!" They looked at each other, smiled and continued singing along with the radio. I repeated, a bit louder, "I have something to tell you!" They turned the radio volume up a little louder and kept singing with The Rolling Stones, "I can't get no satisfaction!" They were having fun with me, in a good way. Eventually I got to share my story with them, but then, they already knew...I didn't really need to tell them.

THE GIFTING

Edie and I got to stay with Norm and Sonja in Ketchikan. I was still reeling with nervous excitement from my Metlakatla experience. They invited us to go to church with them the next day, which we did. The people there warmly greeted us. Prior to this, I had not experienced the nonjudgmental, loving spirit that I felt here, in a church setting. Music worship included hand drum, guitar, and keyboard.

The pastor brought the message, and as he concluded, he said, "Someone here needs to speak," and he looked right at me.

I had never met him or been to this church before. I had not yet even shared my Metlakatla experience with Sonya and Norm. I got up and went to the front where the pastor was, and we shook hands. I introduced myself in the Native way, including stating my heritage and thanking the host people of the land, protocol which I had learned years ago. Then I spoke, after which I returned to my seat beside Edie. I noticed an elder man walk up to the front where I had just spoken. He looked around the room, then his gaze landed on me.

He said, "Standing Bear, come here."

"Oh no! What did I do?" I thought.

He held his hand up and motioned me to come up. When my wobbly legs finally brought me up to him, he put his hand on my shoulder and started speaking in his Tlingit tongue. Many of the attendees were Tlingit from Saxman, but I had no idea what he was saying. When he finished speaking, he proceeded to take the necklace off his neck and place it over my head onto my neck, then touched it gently and smiled.

I returned to my seat and a thought came to me to ask Norm or Sonja to interpret what this elder had said, but immediately, the Spirit of God told me that He knew what the elder said, because He gave him this language, so I did not need an interpretation. I still wear this necklace today, 15 years later.

THE CONCLUSION OF THE MATTER

Who would guess that a cedar plank floating in the ocean, and the drummers and dancers of Metlakatla would help me in my journey in the Jesus Way? The answer to that would be Doug, Guy, Bill, and Richard, and of course, Jesus, all to whom I am eternally grateful.

GETTING OUT OF THE BOX

(Story by Edie Winter Song)

"For it is not those who hear the law who are righteous in God's sight, but it is those who obey the law who will be declared righteous."

Romans 2:13

"Show me where it calls God 'Grandfather,' or where smudging is practiced in the Bible," I challenged.

He became unusually angry and for the only time in our marriage said something about divorce as he walked out the door. I was incredulous. Don and I were arguing about his pursuit of his Native heritage and its associated spirituality. We had been married six years when he decided to begin this journey. I was a member of a small church nearby which taught me that the King James Version was the only acceptable version of the Bible, that drums were not to be used in church, no clapping allowed and certainly no dance expression, and that this denomination was the only right one, among other limitations. I believed them, and I was freaking out that my husband was leaving the faith, and he and I were growing apart. I felt betrayed. I married him because he was a Christian, and now he was determined to become increasingly involved in his Native heritage instead. We were at an impasse.

In stepped God. A mutual friend handed us the book, "One Church, Many Tribes: following Jesus the way God made you." (10) The author, Richard Twiss, is pictured on the cover in his Lakota Sioux traditional Native regalia. This piqued my interest right away. I had an affinity for

Native ways that I had felt guilty about and suppressed, since it was not "acceptable" to God.

Don, of course, let me read the book first, and once I started reading, I couldn't put it down. It spoke to my heart. It spoke truth and answered the questions I had. It gave me peace within my spirit that I had lacked.

Our Creator is a God of diversity. He enjoys worship in all the various cultural expressions. What matters is our personal relationship with Him, not which instrument we play as we worship him, whether we dance or not, or which version of the Bible we read. His Holy Spirit guides us. In fact, in the Bible, Miriam used timbrels, a percussion instrument, and David danced.

The thought came to me that I had been employing the "Spanish Inquisition" mentality when discussing the Bible and Native beliefs with my husband. I had been judgmental, closed minded, and arrogant...not a very good example of Jesus, who I thought I was representing and defending (1 John 4:20: "If a man says he loves God, and hates his brother or sister, he is a liar"). I was operating under a spirit of contention, rather than under the Holy Spirit. I was ashamed. I went and apologized to Don, explaining to him that I had looked at Native beliefs all very literally and superficially from "inside the box" that I was in, instead of seeing the deeper spiritual meaning. I finally understood why he got so angry the day that he had threatened divorce. He had finally embraced who God made him, only to be rejected and mocked by his wife.

I now realized that "Grandfather" is one name used for God, because it is the most highly revered position in Native culture. Smudging involves cleansing and prayer, with the smoke rising to Creator. Priests in the Bible burned incense, symbolizing prayers of the faithful, rising to God.

Richard Twiss' book was life-changing for me. That affinity I had for Native ways was revived, and I recognized that it was their genuine innate connection to Creator, his creation, and to their fellow man, that I admired, and desired to develop in my own spiritual walk. Native Ways and the Jesus Way were not mutually exclusive. They are complementary. Native cultures were often good examples of the Jesus way, with their code of honor and respect for God, each other, and all living things. Jesus was in North America before European contact. He created it and all peoples everywhere and loves us all the same. The Bible has 365 names for God, describing his various attributes. Names such as "Grandfather" and "Great Spirit" in Native language, I am sure, are welcomed by Him. (Revelations 7:9).

Don and I now routinely participate in Native events together, including some Native Jesus Way events, and powwows, Alaska Native dance/drum groups, and other cultural celebrations.

I was gifted the Native name "Winter Song" from my dad-in-law, Grey Wolf.

Don and I have had the honor of spending time with Richard Twiss, and many other Jesus Way Native leaders over the years. I have been blessed to experience so much more joy, peace, love, and unity of the brethren, while celebrating our diversity together (Psalm 133:1: Behold how good and pleasant it is when God's people live together in unity!") I have learned not to limit God to my expectations. He is so much bigger than that! I am so thankful that God helped me to get "out of the box."

> *The evangelist Billy Graham once said, "The greatest moments of Native history may lie ahead of us if a great spiritual renewal and awakening should take place. The Native American has been a sleeping giant. He is awakening. The original Americans could become the evangelists who will help win America for Christ! Remember these forgotten people!" (11) (One Church, Many Tribes, page 24)*

"God is spirit, and they who worship him must worship him in spirit and in truth."

John 4:24

CHAPTER FOUR:

PHYSICAL (strength)

pertaining to the body; of, or pertaining to material nature (12)

SOLUTIONS TO PAIN

"He has chosen not to heal me, but to hold me. The more intense the pain, the closer His embrace."

Joni Eareckson Tada, "A Place of Healing"

My physical stature and behavior earned me the nickname "The Grizz," or "Papa Grizz". I took pride in my physical and mental toughness. I had played professional hockey, worked security for famous performers at concerts, functioned as bouncer at various drinking establishments, participated in socially unacceptable fraternities, won (and usually started) every fight, heated my house with wood, hauled water, and ran sled dogs. I was tough!

I did have my share of physical injuries associated with these activities: stitches, broken bones, concussions. I was no stranger to pain. "No pain, no gain," was my motto. I was selfish, self-centered, and self-reliant. I was the quintessential rugged "Alaskan Man." I considered myself invincible, until......

"I can move this heavy table, no problem! Owww! What just happened?"

A sharp pain shot down my right leg, from my lower back to my toes. I tried to slough it off and continue to work, but I would soon discover that this pain would not be overcome by my usual sheer guts and determination, augmented by generous amounts of alcohol, as had always worked in the past.

The back surgeon told me he could fix it so I "could do anything but gymnastics." I had the surgery, and three more after that, by the same surgeon. None of them worked, and only made matters worse. The fourth surgery lasted six hours instead of the two hours it was scheduled for. During recovery, I became so hypothermic, shivering violently, such that one nurse told me she thought they were going to lose me. I had to spend the next ten days in the hospital. My friends, Jim and Patricia, visited me faithfully. Jim kept saying that something was not right. Neither of us could get an answer from the surgeon.

I had no concept of chronic pain. All my prior injuries and surgeries were just short-lived inconveniences. As the days after that fateful event of May 12, 1983 continued, I became impatient with this current relentless pain situation. I wanted to be done with it and move on to pursuing my lifelong dream of running my dog team in the Open North American Sled Dog Championship Race, the "Granddaddy" of the sprint sled dog racing world, as well as returning to my indestructible "Alaskan Man" status. But that was not meant to be. My life, instead, was irrevocably changed by that fateful one minute in 1983.

Thus began the roller coaster ride on the "pain train", with no conductor, brakeman, nor engineer, which lasted for thirty-three years.

To add insult to injury, since the injury occurred on the job, I had to deal with the workers compensation system bureaucracy, with its myriads of paperwork, attorneys, doctors, physical therapists, and vocational rehabilitation counselors, all who seemed to be paid to work against the injured worker, rather than to help him. I realize there is a certain amount of fraud which they must battle, but this makes it tough for the workers who are genuinely injured.

After several years, I finally was able to convince the Workers Compensation Board to let me seek a second opinion to see if my back was redeemable. My new orthopedic surgeon reviewed my old postoperative x-rays and showed me a foreign object in my spinal canal at the surgical site. He referred me to Mayo Clinic to determine what to do about it. Their team of specialists determined that the foreign object was the broken-off tip of metal curette, an instrument used during back surgeries. They said it was now anchored in scar tissue and further surgery to try to get it out was too risky.

My fate was sealed. This was as good as it was gonna get, and this was not very good. In addition to constant pain, I suffered from "foot drop", numbness and uncontrollable weakness of my right foot and ankle, which had caused me to fall more than once, and even sustain an ankle fracture. Mayo Clinic physical therapists had to teach me how to walk again, and their Pain Clinic counselors taught me techniques to try to deal with the pain, but the pain was too much.

Chronic pain took over my life. It affected every facet, the emotional, mental, and spiritual, as well as the physical. Fear welled up. Run away! Do not bother me! God is punishing me! I lashed out at those around me, then sealed my cocoon of self-pity around me. Hopelessness and depression set in. I could not make plans or commit to anything. I could not even concentrate enough to do simple tasks. I was useless. Dealing with the pain absorbed all my energy. Pain had stolen my life. It became my identity....at least it did for a while.

But along the way, God sent me teachers who shared with me some solutions to pain. Let me share them with you:

Feed the birds:

I was depressed, feeling hopeless and useless. My friend told me to go buy a bird feeder, put it outside the window facing my recliner, and check it each day to keep it full. Once the birds started coming, they would depend on me to keep feeding them. I was able to follow through on this suggestion. But a week later, no birds. Just as I was becoming discouraged, the birds began to appear, one, then two, then many, and every day. They were a joy to watch, and it did my heart good to know that I was making their lives better. I had found purpose, no matter how small. I found something to which I could commit. I forgot about the pain for periods during the day as I enjoyed the birds' activities. Three decades later, we still keep the bird feeder full.

"**When was the last time you forgot about the pain because you were doing something for someone else?**" More words of wisdom from my friend. This time he was referring to people in need, even if just talking on the phone with them, supporting them through their challenges. When I would do this, after we hung up, I realized the pain had not bothered me during our conversation.

Don't isolate; you can't do this alone:

Sometimes I was the one who needed to call my friend for encouragement.

Pain medicine:

Sometimes I had to take it, though I tried to avoid it.

Focus on what you can do, not in what you can't do:

I could not work because of my back pain, but I could help with chores around our house and property. I used to push through to complete tasks before resting, but with pain, I had to learn to take frequent breaks, which allowed me to eventually complete the tasks, rather than giving up entirely.

Go for a walk:

Spend time in creation. Soak in the silence or the songs of the birds, the river, the tree leaves rustling. Enjoy the beauty of the seasons: northern lights, golden leaves, flowers, a walk in the woods.

Advocate for my own well-being:

I learned that I had to take an active role in this. In 2009, I ended up making the decision to spend my winters in Arizona due to the inability to keep my nerve-damaged feet warm in the Alaskan winters. I would either have to sit inside all winter or go somewhere else. It turned out to be a good decision to go somewhere warm for winters.

Read a good book:

A friend handed me the book "Choosing Joy" (13). It proved extremely helpful.

Prayer:

It's okay to pray for relief. The answer comes in diverse ways and various times, often through other people. My spiritual flame flickered sometimes, but never went out.

Do not give up hope:

Something good could happen.

In 2015, God moved in a big way. Based on my symptoms of progressive nerve damage related to my back injury, my neurologist ordered an MRI. My spinal canal was narrowed by 80%. I needed surgery to relieve the compressed nerves, and soon! We prayed, and were able to find a top-rated surgeon in Arizona, who specialized in treating back injuries like mine, and a top-rated hospital he had privileges at.

December 28, 2015, I had the surgery. The next morning, as I carefully maneuvered to the side of the bed and placed my feet on the floor, I turned to my wife and blurted out, "I can feel my right foot!" Tears of gratitude and joy began to flow as I enjoyed that marvelous sensation for the first time in thirty-three years. After the surgical pain diminished, I began to realize my new paradigm. I no longer suffered chronic pain. I was SO thankful. And with renewed sensation in my foot, I needed to relearn how to walk. Now, six years later, I continue to be free of chronic pain, and I can live a normal life. I am forever grateful for how God provided all those who prayed for me, shared their wisdom, and supported me through the tough times, and for that life changing answer to my prayer. I have learned much through my pain journey, which I am now able to share with those still struggling. I pray for a solution for them. Miracles can happen. I am one. Sometimes they take time. Don't give up.

"In the same way, the Spirit helps us in our weakness. We do not know what we ought to pray for, but the Spirit himself intercedes for us through wordless groans...And we know that in all things God works for the good of them who love Him, who have been called according to his purpose."

Romans 8:26,28

MYSTERIOUS MALADY

"... and be content with what you have, because God has said, 'Never will I leave you; never will I forsake you."

Hebrews 13:5

I picked up the phone, and the voice on the other end said, "Are you in your house now? You need to get out, and don't take anything with you!"

What?? Yes, I was in the house, that was where the landline phone I was talking on was located.

I used to joke with my wife that I liked it "cool, dark, and damp," a reflection of my former unhealthy existence, living in the proverbial cave. Watch out what you ask for; you might get it. I had been struggling with all kinds of weird symptoms for a number of years: hearing loss, visual changes, mental decline, and even skin abscesses. I began to suspect that my old god of wrath was judging me for my dark past, and trying to crowd out the true God of love. Depression set in.

My medical doctor put me through rigorous testing: neurologic exams, hearing test, stress test, pulmonary function test, scans, x-rays.... you name it, with no conclusive diagnosis.

A friend suggested seeing a holistic doctor. This was the turning point. She did a thorough assessment: physical, mental, emotional, spiritual, diet, sleep patterns, activity, living conditions, stressors. My symptoms of neurotoxicity and skin abscesses suggested a causative agent. She made arrangements for further testing…not of me, but of my house! The testing was completed within the next couple of weeks.

We lived in an old house which was supported only by cement pilings, with poor drainage which persisted despite all our re-landscaping efforts. Beneath our bedroom resided a mud bog which proved a perfect breeding ground for all seven kinds of mold. Black mold was even visible creeping up the corners of the bedroom behind the bed and in the closet. We had no idea just how toxic this mold was until now! It made sense, God made the mold to break down, decay, and decompose matter for purposes of recycling. Unfortunately, as my holistic doctor had explained, this mold was breaking down and destroying my body, from my cognitive and sensory function, to my immune system, to skin abscesses. I exhibited all the classic symptoms. Her diagnosis was confirmed by the phone call from the mold testing company informing me that our house tested positive for seven types of toxic mold, and we needed to get out immediately!

On the one hand, I was relieved to finally know what was wrong with me. On the other hand, we were suddenly homeless. We had to abandon our home of 25 years with its great collection of artwork and personal effects that were precious to us. We had many fond memories in this, our home, with family and friends, Christmas open houses with the accompanying lavish lights and decorations, connections, love, and laughter. People always said our house was very warm and welcoming. Now it would be no more. With both sadness and gratitude, we left our home.

My wife's coworker had offered to sell us his 1972 C-class Leprechaun camper a few years prior. We bought it, used it only a few times, but mostly roof raked the snow off it every winter. Now we knew why we were led to keep it. My wife and I immediately moved into this little camper. It was mid-summer 2004. I knew we had only a couple of months before the cold and snow moved in, but we were so thankful even for this temporary home where we would be warm and dry.

The help we received from friends could never be repaid. They came and loaded up pickup trucks full of our belongings from the house and brought it all to the dumpsters. Because mold invades any porous surface, we could take nothing from our mold infested house except dishes, pots, pans, and silverware but not much else. Even to do this, we had to wash everything in bleach, and buy an ozone generating device, then enclose these items in a walled-off room for decontamination via exposure to the ozone for 24 hours. So no one would try to recycle anything from the dumpsters, upholstery was slashed, and wood or hard surfaced items were spray-painted with the word "MOLD" on them. I watched my friends destroy our furniture, computer, TV, stereo, artwork, and most of our earthly treasures.

One day my friend turned to me with a tear in his eye and said, "How can you stand there and watch us destroy all your things?"

I responded, "I know what is wrong with me, and this is part of the solution."

My wife, Edie, and I were taking a load of personal items to the dumpster, which included her beautiful wedding dress and my wedding suit. I remember her running her hands over the dress as if to remember the feel of the satin for the last time.

When we were about to toss the items into the dumpster, I told her, "Why don't you throw in my suit, and I will throw your dress in?" She agreed and we tossed them in together.

Meanwhile time marched on and we still needed a real (and warm) home before winter.

In 1994, we had a 30'x32' heated garage built and had the shell of a studio apartment framed in above it but lacked the money to finish it. I had hoped to eventually finish it and rent it, to supplement our income.

Then in 1999, our friend had a horrific accident, where a drunken driver crashed his semi-truck into our friends' parents' car. He was a passenger in the backseat. He suffered multiple injuries and fractures, and both his parents were killed. It took him months to recover. One day he and his wife came to us and offered an interest-free loan from his settlement so we could finish the apartment. We accepted their gracious gift, finished the apartment, and rented it. In July 2004, my nephew was renting it, however, when he learned of our homeless state, he relocated up the street. Then on September 1, we moved into the studio apartment.

We bought a mattress and that was our furniture in our new home. We were thankful to have a non-poisonous, healthy home, with furniture or not! Little by little, friends offered us various furnishings and miraculously, as we measured for each piece it fit exactly right in the limited space. The apartment with its large deck was becoming our home and calling it "the apartment" no longer fit. One day, I was looking out its various windows and I saw sky and trees all around. That inspired its new name, our "Treehouse," and it has become incredibly special to us. We prefer its elevation and brightness to our old house. The old house still stands so the ravens have somewhere to perch and roll moss down the roof until we have money to have it torn down.

My holistic doctor immediately started me on treatment for mold toxicity and explained that complete recovery would take about a year. I had skin abscesses that required surgical removal. It was as if my body was trying to force the mold out through my skin. Treatment involved rounds of IV antibiotics, vitamin C, natural supplements, serial bloodwork, and more. Little by little, over the course of a month, I started feeling better. By 10 months later, my massage therapist told me during an appointment that my skin pores were starting to clear up. I asked what she meant. She told me that my pores had been black, and the mold was finally exiting my body.

Then by the 12-month mark, as predicted by my holistic doctor, all my faculties returned to normal. This mold experience allowed me to better appreciate physical abilities, such as seeing, hearing, and thinking clearly, so much more. It taught me how dangerous mold is, so I share this new-found knowledge with others who may be experiencing similar symptoms. But most of all, the provision of everything needed to identify, treat, and overcome this once mysterious malady — even down to the "coincidental" factor of having the camper immediately available to move into, and then the Treehouse (originally an afterthought during the construction of the garage years earlier), available to move into permanently — reminded me that my Creator was lovingly healing and providing for me, rather than judging me, as I originally thought. I have much to be grateful for.

> *"But I will restore you to health and heal your wounds."*
>
> Jeremiah 30:17

THIS VESSEL

"Where can I go from your Spirit? Where can I flee from your presence? If I say surely the darkness will hide me, and the light becomes night around me, even the darkness will not be dark to you; the night will shine like the day, for darkness is as light to you."

Psalm 139:7,11,12

"What the heck is going on?"

I woke up one morning with a swollen, useless, painful, wrist, with no apparent cause. X-rays revealed that a bone in my wrist was dead (avascular necrosis) and needed to be removed as soon as possible. I reflected on how I had fractured this wrist badly more than once in my hockey goaltending days and had pulled off the cast early so I could play hockey sooner. Now I was reaping the rewards of my poor judgment.

My doctor arranged for me to see a hand specialist in Anchorage, a 45-minute flight away. On the plane, a distressed mom and her adult daughter were sitting near me. The mom was sobbing audibly and appeared to be in some sort of pain. I felt a nudge to ask them if I could pray for them.

"Yes, please do!" implored the daughter.

Though I did not know their circumstances, I prayed for them, which noticeably calmed and comforted them, and they thanked me profusely.

When I arrived at the specialist's office, the receptionist told me that the insurance had not approved the visit yet, so I would have to reschedule. I was not happy. My wrist hurt. I had wasted all that time and expense flying down. Now I would have to do it all over again, after insurance finally approved my visit. Right about then, I recalled my experience on the flight down. Maybe that was what this trip was about, and not about me.

Insurance eventually approved my appointment and surgery, and it all went well, but I was told it would take several months of occupational therapy before I could work again.

Healing, it seemed to me, was terribly slow, as I continued with occupational therapy. I felt useless. I could not work, use the computer, help my wife with kennel chores or around the house, and I couldn't even write, since it was my dominant hand. Constant frustration led to resignation, and finally depression. Why was God not helping? I gave up hope. I just wanted to die.

One day, Edie asked me to meet her for lunch at her work after my occupational therapy appointment. I told her NO! You see, this was my appointed time to do myself in. But Creator God had already put in place other plans for me that day. My plan was to go to my occupational therapy appointment and then have a horrendous car crash.

My occupational therapist sensed there was something wrong with my demeanor and tried to encourage me the best she could. The next thing I knew, I somehow found myself in my therapist's office, telling the receptionist that I wanted to commit suicide. She told me to stay put and returned to inform me that the doctor would see me right away. He gave me some sample medicine that would help at once and told me to return the next day to talk more. After this, I surprised my wife for lunch at her workplace, although I had not changed my secret plans. Despite saying nothing of it to her, she sensed something was not right and expressed her concern. She even said there was a bad spirit about me, and she prayed that I would find help.

At that point I remembered that there was a gathering of sober people going on right then, and I felt the need to go there. When I walked in, a friend greeted me in a shocking way.

She said, "Get over here. I need to pray over you. You have a bad spirit about you." She did just that.

I went into this gathering place and sat down, feeling a darkness that clouded my whole being. I remember voicing a request openly for some men to spend time with me when the meeting ended. There I sat, after the meeting ended with the closing prayer. No men came over. Instead, as the room emptied, two women came over. I knew the immense value of our women "life givers", from my cultural and traditional teachings. What was even more powerful, in this instance, was that one Native, and one non-Native woman came over to me. Each kneeled down, one on either side of me, as I sat slumped in my chair. They each took turns, praying in Athabaskan and English. Their fervent prayers started to lift the dark cloud of despair from my being. Hope started to seep in, assuring me that I would be okay, no matter what.

Then as their tag-teaming prayers continued, I was moved to lift my arms and embrace myself, hugging the vessel Creator God had given my spirit to live in. I had always been critical of this defective, pain-ridden body, never really accepting, and certainly never appreciating it. I was constantly battling with myself until now. A new paradigm of gratitude and peace replaced the depression and hopelessness. I shared this newfound epiphany with the two prayer warriors. We got up and hugged and I thanked them for their prayers. And I thanked my Creator for His working through the people He put in my path that day.

On my drive home, I called my wife. When she heard my voice, she squealed with delight and told me that my voice sounded so good, and she praised Creator God! I drove my newly appreciated vessel home to hug her. My wrist experienced a full recovery, too.

CHAPTER FIVE

VISION QUEST

"Oh, Great Spirit, whose voice I hear in the winds, I come to you as one of your many children. I need your strength and your wisdom. Make me strong, not to be superior to my brother, but to be able to fight my greatest enemy: myself".

Chief Dan George, Coast Salish, 1899–1981

"I can't stay in Alaska in the winter anymore," I told my wife. The compression of the nerves of my legs from my old back injury had reached the point where my feet and lower legs became numb, cold, and discolored in cold weather, as the nerves to the blood vessels no longer functioned properly. I had been told years ago that my back was too messed up to have surgery, so I just had to make the best of it with the way it was.

I talked with my wife, and family and friends to figure out where to go for the winters. My friends Mike and Cindy, who had a home in Arizona, suggested I try wintering there.

In 2008, I had done a couple of Native American art shows in the Southwest, and Mike had taken me out to see the desert in his Jeep. I was like a kid in a candy shop, "Ooh"ing and "Ahhh"ing at the mixture of mountains, sand, rock formations, cactus, and beautiful blue sky. Mike was thoroughly entertained by my sense of wonder. Pictures and videos just did not compare to being there and experiencing this portion of God's creation firsthand! This is where I would snowbird to. Cindy suggested a nice RV park in Wickenburg where she had stayed in the past.

We called and they said, "Sorry, we are full...oh wait! We have one spot left!"

I said, "I'll take it!"

Edie and I bought a pull-behind camper during a trip to Massachusetts, and my dad gave me his hardly used, 1994 Ford F-250 truck to haul it down to Wickenburg.

The RV Park was everything Cindy had promised. The site turned out to have nice neighbors and even a row of multicolored rose bushes! (I still have the same spot, thirteen years later).

During my first season as a snowbird, I was welcomed by my new extended family, and opportunities to expand my horizons as a Native artist presented themselves. Everything was new and exciting! Living in an RV park, enjoying the sunlight and warmth, and the ability to be active outside during the winter months was so refreshing! I felt like this was where I was supposed to be.

In Arizona is where I met Indian Ron. We became friends and he invited me to The Ranch, a treatment facility for those seeking recovery from drug and alcohol abuse. Located about 9 miles off the highway outside of Wickenburg, it was also an active cattle ranch, where clients worked during recovery. We met in town, and I followed his truck down the dusty dirt road, heading for our destination. The day, sunny and comfortably warm, was typical March weather for this area. As Ron drove across the dry washes and up-and-down endless hills, I begin to feel doubtful and nervous, and at intervals, thought about turning around to head back to the comfort of the known. But God seemed in control of my gas pedal and steering wheel, and there was no turning back. The thought, not my own, ran through my mind: "I have the message you need, to help you on this journey."

My thoughts were interrupted when Ron suddenly pulled over. We had arrived at The Ranch. Ron continued to a path that leads down to the Hassayampa River. There, with dust floating all around from the drive, we exited our vehicles.

Ron pointed. "There it is." He had set up a tipi lodge as a place of spiritual retreat and teaching, offering a diversion from the stone and wood western style buildings that housed clients.

He turned and walked away, leaving me to my own instincts as to how to proceed, on this, my Vision Quest. I had been whisked away from the distractions of the outside world. I looked around at the barns and stables, and the bunk houses used by the young adults seeking recovery. The spirit of healing here was almost palpable. The immaculate appearance of the place reflected its worth to those who stayed and worked here.

I peered down the path towards the distant tipi lodge, my destination. I would have to cross a river, and then face the next unusual challenge which I could see from this vantage point. Fear told me to hesitate, but determination and faith prodded me on. I would need to make several trips out to the lodge with everything I would need for my sojourn there. I may as well get started. Loaded up with my first batch of supplies, I moved to the river's edge. With the chronic numbness in my right foot, I had to routinely watch my step.

I looked across the clear running water and estimated there to be about fifty feet of wetness to traverse in order to reach the other side. I cautiously placed one foot at a time. I could feel the kiss of the cool, rushing water on my legs. The sunlight glinted off the mix of sand and stone at the river's bottom. I was relieved to find the water more shallow than expected. It was just up to my knees, and I traversed it with no major difficulty. With soggy shoes and wet pants, I emerged from the river. Waiting for me was a herd of large, intimidating looking Longhorn steers. A number of them walked toward me with their gaze set on this intruder who dared to disrupt their serenity.

"What do I do now?" I asked Creator!

Ancestral wisdom and instinct kicked in, "Speak gently: they will not harm you," came the answer. So as the steers and I were checking each other out, I prayed over them, goodness, gentleness, and trust. They responded in kind, and respectfully made way for me to continue my journey. I slowly proceeded down the path that led to the tipi lodge. About a quarter mile later, the path opened to where I would be granted the much sought-after wisdom from Creator God.

I entered the lodge with my first load of supplies, along with excitement and anticipation. After two more round trips through the now-disinterested steers, across the cool river and back, I was ready to tune-in, in preparation for whatever God had for me to experience.

The location of the lodge was ideal. There were a few trees, thanks to the nearby water source, some scrub brush and numerous oases of grasses dotted the landscape. To the south were hills, with steep drop offs from their majestic bluffs which seem to stretch from horizon to horizon. To the west, flowed the river, boundary to yet another bluff, again with a steep drop off. The tipi lodge itself was large (I later learned it could hold twenty-five people comfortably). Because of my back problems, I had chosen to haul out a "traditional" zero gravity lawn chair. I set up my chair inside the lodge and took a short time-out prior to starting preparation for the reason I came. As I sat there, looking out through the opening of the lodge, it came to me that I needed to set up outside to be in the sunlight of the Spirit. I moved the chair outside. Now I was ready.

A good portion of the supplies that I had brought with me represented the basic tools I had used in my spiritual journey. I prayed as I unpacked. Prayer was always a good place to begin. Next, I decided to focus on the first gift God had given me in my spiritual walk. I began reading from my sobriety books and from the Bible. Then I reflected on the cultural teachings from my Native heritage. These sources of spiritual inspiration and wisdom harmonize well, and together give me a sense of wholeness of who God made me. Still praying, I mixed sacred tobacco, sage, cedar, and sweet grass in my abalone shell. Then I set it aflame and extinguished it down to a smolder, fanning it with my eagle feather. I prayed, facing the seven directions, one at a time, beginning with the East, then South, West, and North. Then I lifted my eyes to the heavens and prayed for God's guidance and lowered my head to look to the earth and prayed gratitude for God's Creation and provision. Finally, I pivoted in a circle, to thank Creator for all my relations: animal, plant, the winged ones, the swimming ones, rock, and mineral. I leaned down and carefully unwrapped my hand drum and sprinkled some sacred tobacco on the head of the drum as I prayed gratitude. This drum's heartbeat brings me connection with the living earth around me. I smiled as I thought of how probably every culture has a drum. Four strong drumbeats break the silence, resonating across the river valley, in honor of the four directions. My first song is the Mi'kmaq Honor Song, followed by songs dedicated to my Quest.

Now I felt ready and willing to "just be". My lawn chair beckoned and I answered. As I got comfortable, I couldn't help but stop and take in my surroundings again. Some small birds fluttered around from bush to bush. I contemplated the surrounding hills, the movement of the cattle, and the gurgling of the flowing river. My spirit was soothed. Serenity. My eyes started to close, and my mind calmed yet further. Relax. Breathe. Be in the moment.

I focused on the faint sound of the water, bringing a deeper peace. My breathing was slow and deliberate. I could feel my heartbeat in my chest and my blood course through my veins. My heart felt like it had perfect rhythm with the breath of my lungs. I had not before felt this tuned in and at peace with the world around me, and within myself. I felt fully comfortable in my own skin, for the first time, at least the first time to this depth. It was divine. I was open, receptive, teachable.

I believe God, as we relate to Him, will send messengers and messages in ways that we can understand. With me, he sometimes uses a mind's-eye "billboard". I was about to receive such a billboard message.... the answer to my Vision Quest, but it was a startlingly simple and almost humorous message considering all my deep and serious preparation. The message was clear and bold: "IT'S NOT ABOUT YOU!" I started to chuckle, the humor of God! I couldn't help but laugh at myself. The great wisdom I had set about to learn with this whole experience was so remarkably wonderful. It's not about me! The joy in this truth that I felt, words cannot describe.

I opened my eyes and there were two individuals in the distance walking towards me. I recalled that Ron had mentioned he may send out a couple of young men to visit with me. Again, I just laughed in my spirit, waiting for their arrival. A deeper comprehension of "it's not about me", was beginning to blossom...and to do so immediately! But my lesson did not end there. There was to be more....

As the two men approached me, I noticed a remarkable contrast between the two. The first to speak was articulate and expressed hope for his new life. Conversation came easily to him. He had some recovery under his belt. The second young man appeared lost and distant. I learned that drug use had caused severe damage to his body, mind, and spirit. But he was here, seeking life. All I could do was encourage his road to recovery. I remember an overwhelming feeling of compassion for him. We talked about our lives and hope, and as our time together came to a close and they got up to head back across the river to the ranch, the first young man told me that Ron gave him a message to pass on to me. I was to come up to the dining hall for dinner at 5 PM.

At 5 PM, as I approached the dining hall, I was greeted by a friend from Wickenburg who works as a counselor at the Ranch. It was good to see him. He walked with me into the hall. The whole place was buzzing with activity, as the men were setting tables and preparing the meal. The teamwork and care they displayed working their given tasks impressed me and evoked a feeling of gratitude within me. How many of these young men started off empty and lifeless, much like my visitor today? Now comradery, laughter, and life were gifted to them. They were given hope, and I was given hope for them. This trip was no longer about me. It was about these young men.

During dinner, my counselor friend informed me that for the next couple of hours he and I would make ourselves available to visit with these young men, and then I would be sharing my story that evening at the fire pit meeting. Then I would be another hour or so in the lounge, to spend more time with the clients.

When I had arrived that morning for my Vision Quest, I had no interest in working with young adults. I have always worked with adults and elders in recovery from trauma and addictions and avoided young adults, just not my thing. When Creator told me that it's not about me, out there at the tipi lodge, He had arranged to let me know, with no delay, just who then it was about.

Just those few hours before, Creator had opened my eyes, ears, mind, and heart, and I became open-minded. Now, as these young adults and I spoke of our joys and struggles and shared our hearts, I started to learn how to love these young men who were so earnestly seeking healing from their addictions, just as their Creator loved them. I experienced a paradigm shift. This was a turning point in my life and ministry.

As the evening's activities and visiting with the clients ended, another friend who was a counselor there, asked me to accompany him to the staff bunkhouse so we could talk. The sky was dusky and the first stars visible, as we entered the staff residence. We were like kids at a slumber party. We were too energized to sleep. We sat and conversed about the spiritual journey we were each on until the wee hours of the morning. When sleep finally came to us, there was only time for a short nap.

Then, as the Arizona sun crept over the horizon I awoke, physically spent, yet spiritually charged. I thanked Creator for granting me HIS vision, the answer to my vision quest. Now it was time for me to retrieve my belongings from the lodge across the river and to return to

Wickenburg. As I waded across the river, I heard a tractor coming down the pathway I had just walked. I figured they must have chores to do with the Longhorns. As I reached the lodge, I looked back to see the tractor with two of the young men heading right towards where I was sorting through my belongings, in preparation for the multiple trips back across the river. When the tractor reached the lodge, one of them told me they had come to load me out.

How did anyone know I was leaving? In my sleep deprived exhaustion, I was delighted for the help! We loaded all my belongings into the bucket and headed back down the trail to the river. As we approached the water crossing, one of them told me to hop on.

Something told me it was important for me to return the way I had come, walking through the water, only this time with the vision Creator God had given me. I walked back through the water, a new man. Thus began the next chapter of my spiritual journey and continuing ministry with these, and more, now beloved, young adults.

OUTRO

OUT OF DARKNESS TO LIGHT

"In Him was life, and that life was the Light of all mankind. The light shines in the darkness, and the darkness has not overcome it."

John 1:4,5

These are but a few of the stories of my journey from darkness to light, from my mistaken identity to my true identity, a beloved child of God. You likely have experienced both worlds, including mistaken identity in your life, to some degree. As warriors in two worlds, we all carry quivers full of arrows. Some arrows like anger, blame, and self-deprecation, are weapons of darkness, and destroy us and those around us. Others, like arrows of love, respect, and truth, are weapons of light. They enable us to see ourselves and others as God sees us. We accumulate these arrows through our life experiences, but also through our own decisions, including the realization that we cannot cure ourselves. Self-will cannot overcome destructive self-will. We must get to where we are willing to seek help. Creator is there, waiting for us to open the door, even just a crack, that his light may begin to shine in.

"Behold, I stand at the door and knock. If anyone hears my voice and opens the door, I will come in…" Revelations 3:19-20

Creator knows each of us intimately, before we ever know Him. He knows us better than we know ourselves. Early in my transition from the broken road to the good road, I adopted the beliefs and values of a mentor whom I admired, instead of putting my dependence on my Creator. I did not recognize this until later...something to be aware of in your spiritual walk.

Three of the arrows of darkness which Creator helped me replace in my quiver, were alcohol, feeling rejected by God, and feeling rejected by my fellow man. Alcohol promised a better life. It lied. I thought God had written me off as hopeless, so I had to find my own way. That was a lie. And as a mixed blood, I was a reject in both the Native and non-Native circles. That was a lie. I am now loved and welcomed in both circles.

"You will know the truth and the truth will set you free." John 8:32

Creator knows the specific path each of us must travel, to walk the good road to health and wholeness, and which arrows of light to place in our quivers to replace our arrows of darkness. On my path, He led me to the sobriety movement first, followed by the Jesus Way, and finally, through my First Nations Native ways of wisdom. My cup is overflowing. Now I use these arrows of light to help pierce the armor of darkness of those who Creator puts in my path, or more accurately stated, I show up to let Creator work through me. The gifts of inspiration, hope, encouragement, and love, that were shared with me, are given to be shared with others.

RETREAT

"You are the light of the world. A town built on a hill cannot be hidden. Neither do people light a lamp and put it under a bowl. Instead, they put it on its stand, and it gives light to everyone in the house. In the same way, let your light shine before others that they may see your honorable deeds and glorify your Father in heaven."

Matthew 5:14-16

Many years ago, at a men's spiritual retreat, I had just finished a session working with my mentor, reading and praying, based on "improving (my) conscious contact with God... knowledge of his will for (me), and the power to carry that out." (14) Then he and I, and a number of men he had invited, prayed the Saint Francis of Assisi prayer together (see "Selected Prayers" section of this book). My Osage mentor then opened his Bible and read from Matthew 5:14-16. He emphasized verse 16: "in the same way let your light shine before others that they may see your honorable deeds and glorify your Father in heaven."

He then said, "You need to go for a walk now. As you go, know where the light in you comes from."

I stepped out into the frosty, cold winter's night, clutching my books and Bible on my chest and began walking. The air was clear and crisp. The sky was clear. The stars were shining brightly, and the northern lights were dancing in their rainbow of colors. I came to a spot along the path, and I perceived in my soul, this is a good place. With tears of gratitude running down my cheeks, and freezing on my skin, I spread out my arms, looked to the heavens, and proclaimed, "God, look what you have done!"

PONDERISMS

- Never stop seeking and searching.
- Become teachable.
- Do I inspire or do I bribe?
- Do not act without praying; do not pray without action
- Am I responsible, and to whom?
- Am I criticizing God's handiwork (another person)?
- Do I go to work for a paycheck or to do God's will?
- It's not about me.
- Desire God's will.
- Where is your happy place?
- Realization. Consideration. Action.
- In the Spirit.
- We are all related.
- Want what you have, rather than trying to get what you want.
- Touch the earth: Connect.
- Live life as a prayer.
- Be still. Breathe. Feel your heartbeat. Hear your heartbeat.
- Expect nothing, be grateful for everything.
- Listen: Nature's symphony!
- Practice, practice, practice.
- Freedom of dignity of choice.
- Just for today.
- How's your heart?
- This too shall pass.
- Respectful communication: "Have you considered?"

- My opinion can kill someone; my experience can help heal someone.
- Am I pursuing or am I receiving?
- Embrace the chaos.
- I cannot manipulate Creator God.
- Don't trust me; let me earn your trust.
- Difficult conversation? "Good or bad, right or wrong, this is how I feel."
- Need an attitude change? Do a Blessings/Gratitude list.

SELECTED PRAYERS

The Native American Prayer:

"Oh, Great Spirit, whose voice I hear in the winds, and whose breath gives life to all the world- hear me – I come before you, one of your children. I am small and weak. I need your strength and wisdom. Let me walk in beauty and make my eyes ever behold the red and purple sunset. Make my hands respect the things You have made, my ears sharp to hear Your voice.

Make me wise, so that I may know the things You have taught my people, the lesson You have hidden in every leaf and rock. I seek strength, not to be superior to my brothers, but to be able to fight my greatest enemy, myself. Make me ever ready to come to You, with clean hands and straight eyes, so when life fades as a fading sunset, my spirit may come to You without shame."

Prayer by Yellow Hawk, Sioux Chief

Prayer of Saint Francis of Assisi:

"Lord, make me a channel of Thy peace,

That where there is hatred, I may bring love.

That where there is wrong, I may bring the spirit of forgiveness.

That where there is discord, I may bring harmony.

That where there is error, I may bring truth.

That where there is doubt, I may bring faith.

That where there is despair, I may bring hope.

That where there are shadows, I may bring light.

That where there is sadness, I may bring joy.

Lord, grant that I may seek, rather to comfort, than to be comforted.

To understand, than to be understood.

To love, than to be loved.

For it is by self-forgetting that one finds.

It is by forgiving that one is forgiven.

It is by dying that one awakens to eternal life."

Amen, Aho

Prayer by Johnny "Paleface" (Navajo)

(Looking toward the East) ...

"Creator in the East, Creator of Mother Earth, and the Universe, I am looking to the East, where the sun rises, and the day begins. I have opened my eyes to another day. Please help me by taking away all that is negative. Take away my impatience, intolerance, resentment, denials, anxiety, and all other things that are negative within me."

(Looking towards the South) ...

"Creator in the South, Creator of Mother Earth, and the Universe. I am looking to the South where the sun never sets, and everything grows. Please help me by letting me grow in eyesight and hearing so I can hear and see the beauty you have created. Let me grow in strength, not to be greater than my brother, but to fight my greatest enemy— myself. Please let me grow in wisdom so I can pass it on to others."

(Looking towards the West)

"Creator in the West, Creator of Mother Earth, and the Universe. I am looking to the West, where the sun sets, and the harvest takes place. Let me harvest all that I asked you to take away in the East, so that I can serve you better, by giving me patience, tolerance, and peace of mind. All the things which I asked you to take away, let me have them in the positive so that I can redeem myself in your eyes."

(Looking towards the North) ...

"Creator in the North, Creator of Mother Earth, and the Universe. I am looking to the North. I know that the trail from the South to the North is very long, and as is life, very difficult. Difficult because when you breathed the breath of life into me, you gave me free will. I have used, abused, and misused that will. Now I am ready to do your will. I pray for knowledge of your will for me and the power to carry that out."

"Creator, I know that each day that I open my eyes to the East, I have one more day to redeem myself. Please let me keep this day. Each day I take one more step towards the day that I will be with you, my body will be in Mother Earth, and my spirit will be with you. Let me keep this day so when I am called to you, I can come home to you with clean hands and straight eyes, so that when my life fades, as the fading sunset, my spirit can come without shame."

"Life is a full circle where one never leaves, from birth till the day we cross over. One must live within the circle that the Creator has given to each of us.

> *"These are my words. You can use what words you wish."*

Johnny "Paleface" (Navajo)

THE LORD'S PRAYER, First Nations Version: Matthew 6:9-15

"Instead, when you send your voice to the Great Spirit, here is how you should pray:

Oh, Great Spirit, our Father from above, we honor your name as sacred and holy. Bring your good road to us, where the beauty of your ways in the spirit world above is reflected in the earth below. Provide for us day by day- the elk, the buffalo, and the salmon. The corn, the squash, and the wild rice. All the things we need for each day. Release us from the things we have done wrong, in the same way we release others for the things done wrong to us. Guide us away from the things that tempt us to stray away from your good road and set us free from the evil one and his worthless ways. Aho! May it be so."

A NOTE ON THE COVER DESIGN

My Native mentor and teacher in the Wampum Way, Lynn "Chiwabiinonquay" Bessette, (Strong East Wind Woman), (Mohawk/Wampanoag), a mixed blood like me, returned from conducting wampum-weaving and cultural workshops in Reserves in Canada. While there, she received inspiration for the design, "Warrior in Two Worlds." The wampum bracelet on the cover of this book reflects this design, which she passed on to me. It features red and white separated by a black "warrior" pattern. She envisioned the red and white warrior walking in balance between the two worlds, really a vision for all people, as we are all warriors in two worlds.

The medicine wheel pictured features a Cross within it. Traditional First Nations/Native American beliefs and traditional ways of life closely reflect biblical teachings.

> *" ...when Gentiles, who do not have the law, do by nature things required by the law...they show that the requirements of the law are written on their hearts..."*
>
> Romans 2:14-15

Finally, the stinky trash with old alcohol bottles is rather self-explanatory. That was the starting point of my story.

EPILOGUE

"We discover that we do receive guidance for our lives to just about the extent that we stop making demands upon God to give it to us on order and on our terms. Almost any experienced (person in recovery) will tell how his affairs have taken remarkable and unexpected turns for the better as he tried to improve his conscious contact with God. He will also report that out of every season of grief or suffering, when the hand of God seemed heavy or even unjust, new lessons for living were learned, new resources of courage were uncovered, and that finally, inescapably, the conviction came that God does 'move in a mysterious way His wonders to perform.'"

"Twelve Steps and Twelve Traditions" (15)

FOOTNOTES

1. Alcoholics Anonymous, page 55
2. Webster Dictionary
3. Webster Dictionary
4. Webster Dictionary
5. Our Daily Bread Devotional
6. Alcoholics Anonymous, page 55
7. Webster Dictionary
8. One Church, Many Tribes
9. Alcoholics Anonymous, page 53
10. One Church, Many Tribes
11. One Church, Many Tribes, page 24
12. Webster Dictionary
13. Choosing Joy
14. Alcoholics Anonymous, page 59
15. Twelve Steps and Twelve Traditions, page 104-105

BIBLIOGRAPHY

"Alcoholics Anonymous" copyright 1976, Alcoholics Anonymous World Services, Inc

Hansel, Tim, "Choosing Joy", copyright 1985, David C Cook Publishing Company

"First Nations Version: An Indigenous Translation of the New Testament" copyright 2021, Rain Ministries Inc. Intervarsity Press

"Life Application Study Bible; New International Version", copyright 2011, Zondervan

"The Living Webster Encyclopedic Dictionary of the English Language,"

Copyright 1977; English Language Institute of America, Inc.

Jean, Terri, "365 Days of Walking the Red Road" copyright 2003; Adams Media

"Twelve Steps and Twelve Traditions," copyright 1985 Alcoholics Anonymous World Services, Inc.

Twiss, Richard, "One Church, Many Tribes"

Wiconi Publishing copyright 2000, by Richard Twiss (Regal Books)

Made in the USA
Middletown, DE
03 September 2024